We Can Do Better, America:

The Case for a New American Party

By Adam Graham

ISBN: 9781686756641

If there's a fire you're trying to douse
You can't put it out from inside the house
—"Washington on Your Side" from the musical *Hamilton*

I didn't leave the Democratic Party, it left me.
—Ronald Reagan

… the United States is for the moment left
with two authoritarian populist parties.
—Kevin Williamson.

Introduction

I recall the day I first identified with the Republican Party. I came from a family where neither parent voted. I was a home-schooled kid who'd become enraptured with politics. The more that I read about the Republican Party, the more I realized their values aligned with my beliefs. The GOP was pro-life and fought for the unborn. Then, a group of Republican freshmen Congressmen on Capitol Hill was charging hard and revealing the utter corruption of the long-serving Democratic Majority.

This affinity for the Republican Party didn't come from my parents. Neither were registered voters at the time. My dad had last cast a protest vote in 1968 for the joke campaign of Pat Paulsen. In 1980, both had registered to vote to cast their ballots for Jimmy Carter but hadn't done it. In the summer of 1991, I declared I was a Republican. This could have been a passing fancy like a kid declaring he was a vegan, but it stuck.

I devoured talk radio and political books. I was introduced to a Republican Party that was the party of big ideas, big ideas that would get our nation away from ruinous deficits and debts. Welfare reform, school choice, respect for individual liberty, and power being returned to the states excited me. These were ideas I believed with all my heart would make our country better by reducing the power of "Big Government" and giving us all more control over our own lives.

I marched in parades and manned fair booths. I trounced through all sorts of weather carrying Republican literature.

I moved into adulthood and my passion for the GOP continued. I gave small contributions to Republican candidates. I ran for office twice. I served as a precinct captain in two states and I was elected Flathead County Montana Party Secretary in 2002. I was a delegate to the Idaho State Party Convention in 2008 and I worked for three Republican Presidential campaigns.

Now, I wasn't naïve enough to be a happy Republican. The Republicans who had railed against big government quickly fell in love with big spending. They had no sooner established responsible spending caps in the 1990s than they were ready to start breaking them. I called the GOP out when they were wrong and that was frequently.

Yet, I remained with the GOP. The Republicans stood for some principles without compromise. The GOP didn't engage in identity politics and the GOP didn't set one American against another. I was outraged by the Democrat's practice of stirring up racial strife to maintain their political power.

The GOP also remained a voice for clean government. When a politician behaved disgracefully, they were dealt with quickly. Senator Bob Packwood (R-OR) resigned in 1995 and Senator John Ensign (R-NV) resigned in 2011 after the GOP threatened to expel them. Meanwhile Democrats allowed obvious miscreants to remain in office and serve as high-powered committee chairmen. That didn't matter. Republicans demanded a high standard of ethics from their leaders and the importance of character.

I remember the day Republican Party left me: May 3, 2016 when Donald Trump won the Indiana Primary. Early on the morning of November 9 2016, after Donald Trump was elected President of the United States, I accepted that the GOP was his party, not mine.

While Donald Trump was the catalyst for my decision to leave the Republican Party, I want to be clear this book isn't principally about him and his outrages. This book is about us and the type of country we want to live in.

Most discussions of American politics have centered around one man ever since he came down the elevator at Trump Tower to announce his candidacy. Trump provokes reactions ranging from the blind adoration of Trump's cult-like followers to the equally blind rage of Trump's most hateful critics.

One ex-Republican critic of Trump declared Trump's polices make the United States worse than Cuba and Venezuela. Both countries are third-world dictatorships where the people's only option for getting rid of bad leaders is an armed revolt. To infer Trump is worse than third-world dictators shows rage has warped critics' sense of reality.

Most modern political talking heads aim to terrify you and get your blood boiling. It's how blogs attract followers, how talk radio holds listeners, and how political writers churn out best-sellers. These tactics can have nasty side effects, like despair, so I refuse to take that approach. This book instead offers you hope.

While we seek together to understand the problems we face, I will show how these problems present us an opportunity to move our country's politics in a better direction. I will also recognize President Trump is only a symptom of larger issues with our nation's politics.

This book is for you if:

- If the current state of politics leaves you repulsed by both parties.
- If you look at our country's strife between whites and minorities, rich and poor, men and women, and say, "We cannot go on like this."
- If you are tired of friendships and families being torn apart by politics.
- If you worry about the future we're creating for the next generation.

This book is not for you if:

- You think our political climate is fine.
- You feel your party's or identity group's uncivil behavior is an appropriate response to the other side's inappropriate behavior.
- You use "Fake News" to mean sources slamming the President as embarrassing and untrustworthy and only trust sources that affirm Trump as "Best President ever!"
- If you wake up every morning and salute a life-sized cutout of the President.

That said, this book is not about beating you up over whoever you voted for in 2016. For many voters, 2016 was a choice of the lesser of two evils. According to CNN's exit poll, one out of four Trump voters voted for him despite believing he lacked the temperament to be President. I voted third party in accord with my conscience. I respect that many voters' consciences dictated they choose between Trump and Clinton. This book hopes to prevent Americans from having to face such a choice ever again.

While this book is about the future, we're going to learn from the past, per the example of the Founding Fathers. When drafting the Constitution, our Founders studied republics throughout history: those that had succeeded to some degree and how they had all eventually failed. They took lessons from history that they used to draft our Constitution.

In advocating for the Constitution in the Federalist Papers, Alexander Hamilton, James Madison, and John Jay spent several letters examining the deficiencies of the then-current form of government under the Articles of Confederation. In a similar way, we'll examine the problems with the Republican Party, the Democrats, and other third parties. This is not to be negative, but to highlight matters we ought to be aware of in establishing a new party.

I will outline an active approach to form a new American political party and how I believe it can succeed where many have failed. I offer my perspective as a lifelong student of American politics and a former activist and officeholder within the Republican Party who has seen how that party functions and observed the failings of other third-party efforts.

Founding a political party involves a lot of demanding tasks. Some of you may not have time to collect signatures to get a party on the ballot, let alone organize a precinct or chair a state party. Some of you may not have the budgets to contribute much financially. Regardless, this book can help you avoid wasting your limited resources.

Some party may come along, regaling you with exciting ideas that resonate with you. This book will help you identify if a new party has an effective plan and organization. If they don't, they aren't worth a minute of your time or a dime of your money. By knowing what a smart party needs to do, you can steer clear of those who are only going to drain you and leave you disappointed. More importantly, it can help you know when a party is worth what time and effort you can offer to help make our country better.

America faces great challenges, and we don't have time to waste on the movements going nowhere. So let's get started reviewing the case for a new conservative party, after which I will in part two reveal a plan for how to establish one successfully.

It's the Parties, Not the System

In beginning this endeavor, you may expect that I'll spend much time railing against the evils of the two-party system as most advocates for third parties do. That's not my approach at all.

To be sure, most States do throw unreasonable hurdles in the front of third parties and independent candidates. Ballot access laws are often unfair and need reformed. It is in America's best interests to make it easier for new parties to form and to gain ballot access. However, multi-party systems are no panacea or otherwise a guarantee of improvement.

Some third world nations have dozens of political parties and no sane American would change places with a citizen of those countries. There is no correlation between a greater number of political parties and nations being happier, freer, or less prone to government corruption.

In addition, in many multi-party systems, only two parties lead the country. Not even party loyalists expect a leader of the Liberal Democrats or the Scottish Nationalist Party to become Prime Minister of the United Kingdom.

The UK's prime minister is always the leader of the Conservative or the Labour party. The only way any of these other parties have a significant role is if no party wins a majority, in which case they may be invited into a coalition.

In Israel, after each election, the Prime Minister has to cobble together a coalition from the various political parties to govern. The current government of Binyamin Netanyahu contains six different political parties and the opposition's coalition contains nine separate parties.

Countries with multi-party systems divide people that would be Democratic or Republican in America amongst several smaller parties. In many ways, America's two major parties operate like two permanent coalitions. This saves on the fuss and delay that other countries deal with.

A two-party system is not prescribed by the Constitution. In fact, many Founding Fathers wanted no political parties, a point we'll discuss in a later chapter. A two-party system is simply practical due to the electoral college. If we had three or more major parties all winning electoral votes, it would throw the election to Congress, perhaps on a regular basis. The people would be so outraged if Congress picked the president instead, this is an outcome to avoid at all costs.

If we had two functional major parties, with freedom for minor parties and independents to exist, that would be a good political system that would work. In fact, it has worked within America's Constitutional framework.

The problem is the major parties are corrupt, dysfunctional, and hopelessly broken. This problem dwarfs the solution of third-party advocates who argue we should have more choices.

The idea of more choices at the ballot box is popular. Since 2006, Gallup has shown majority or near majority support for the formation of a new third party, with 57% supporting the idea in 2016. However, that support is not a motivating factor in people's votes. Over 90% of voters voted for a major party nominee for President. What's the disconnect? The answer can be found in The Declaration of Independence.

The Founding Fathers laid out why they decided to leave Great Britain and also explained why they worked for over a decade to avoid that. "Mankind are more disposed to suffer, while evils are sufferable, than to right themselves by abolishing the forms to which they are accustomed."

The problem with moving to a multi-party system is the two-party system is a familiar form for the American people. "It might be nice to have some more parties," won't convince people to take firm action against the two-party system. A much stronger argument is needed.

Both the Republicans and the Democrats undermine our standing in the world and our battle against terrorism, though in different ways. Both parties are leading us on a road to fiscal disaster, and both are undermining any hope of national unity and respect. Both are noxious, corrosive forces in our culture, out to advance their own power at any cost. The continued domination of the Republicans and Democrats is becoming an insufferable evil, as the Founders would have put it.

The ultimate goal should not be to build parties to compete with them but to consign the current major parties to the ash heap of history. Preferably within the space of a few election cycles.

Such a drastic step has many reasonable arguments against it. The founders in the Declaration reflect the explanation for separation from Great Britain should be given out of a "decent respect for the opinions of mankind." What might those opinions be even among those who fully understand the poisonous effect of the current GOP on our Republic? Imagine those who share these concerns gathered together.

"This is too hard. Presidents come and Presidents go, but parties endure. Remember the early 2000s when Bush was universally loved by the Republicans? What's happened to his reputation now? We need to fight a long-term battle for the soul of the Republican Party. We may even be able to get Trump defeated in a primary."

"You're wrong. The GOP needs punished. I'm staying home for the midterms. Heck, maybe we should vote with the Democrats for a while. That'll shake the GOP up."

"Both major parties have showed how unfit they are, but I don't get this business about new parties. There are third parties already in existence that you can join."

"Forget about parties. The Founding Fathers were right. We should not have any parties at all and just run Independent candidates."

These are worthwhile points to address. Before I get into explaining how to create a new party, I will talk about why a new party is the best hope for America's political future.

Chapter 1
He Didn't Start the Fire
—But He Poured Gasoline On It

All things being equal, it is easier to influence an existing party rather than it is to form a new one. This is why I continued to identify with the Republican Party for many years despite the many problems I had with them.

It would be unfair to blame all of the Republican Party's troubles on Donald Trump. The GOP's problems go back decades. President Trump has simply made many of them more acute to such a degree it's hard to see the GOP's image ever recovering.

What are the GOP's problems? Simply put, in the pursuit of power, they have betrayed Conservatives' core values.

When I first identified as a Republican in the 1990s, the GOP stood for limited government and fiscal responsibility, a sound foreign policy, traditional values, and ethics in government. Fiscal responsibility has long taken a beating. Republicans retook Congress in 1994 promising to balance the budget and reign in spending. They managed to balance the budget thanks to revenue from the .com boom, but began breaking their agreed-upon spending caps while Newt Gingrich was the Speaker of the House.

Gingrich introduced House Republicans to the art of earmarking, inserting pet projects into appropriations bills, usually in corrupt and legally dubious ways. This process grew into the disgrace of Congressmen directing federal funds to wasteful and inappropriate pet projects to curry favor and ensure their own re-election.

Their over-indulgent spending in the late 1990s set the stage for massive deficits in the early 2000s. When Republicans held both houses of Congress, they made excuses for high deficits. Then in 2008, during the financial crisis, Republicans joined Democrats in a lavish bailout of big businesses, a massive government intervention in the economy by the party that once preached market economics.

Republicans, even less principled ones, knew this was the wrong thing to do, but they buckled under pressure from big business. Then-House Minority leader John Boehner urged his caucus to support this bill even though it was a "crap sandwich." Over the coming decade, such became a regular menu item that Congressmen swallowed regularly.

The bailouts have left a bad taste in the mouths of ordinary Americans. Republicans looked like the party that bailed out the rich but opposed bailing out ordinary Americans.

This failure to live up to the promise of fiscal responsibility continued with the GOP's unwillingness to keep its campaign promises on issues such as repealing Obamacare. To be fair, many voters had unrealistic expectations of what could be done by a Republican Congress with a Democratic president. However, these expectations were a result of promises lawmakers made to get elected. So the blame lies with the Republicans for deceiving the voters against Obamacare.

The Republicans came to power in 1994, in part on the out-of-touch, unethical Democratic Congress of the early 1990s, exposing their cheating of taxpayers in the House Post Office and House Bank scandals. The Bill Clinton Administration had a record-breaking number of Independent Counsels that investigated allegations against Clinton and several cabinet-level secretaries. This made the GOP the party of those demanding clean government in 1994.

Yet it took little more than a decade for the GOP to become as rotten as the Democrats had become over forty years. The 2006 Congressional elections went south for Republicans in part due to ethics scandals involving bribery, sexual affairs with underage pages, and the influence peddling of lobbyist Jack Abramoff.

After retaking Congress in 2010, Republicans have never recovered their ethical white knight status. The best of the class of 1994 took pledges to limit their terms and have kept them. The Republicans who have been in Congress since 1994 have been corrupted. Any desire they once had for reform, smaller government, and a responsive government has been replaced by a desire to remain in office. The Republican Congress is full of Golems whose certificates of election are the "precious" that they each hold onto at all costs.

So President Trump isn't the source of the Republican Party's problems. Rather, he is the result of them and exacerbates them beyond repair.

Trump has signed a big tax cut and has taken strong steps on regulatory reform. However, he has done nothing to check Congress' spending spree. President Trump lived up to his nickname as the King of Debt and signed a budget resolution that sets us on a path of trillion-dollar deficits for as far as the eye can see.

President Trump's messaging is inconsistent, alarming, and deleterious. He's sided with the Russians against our nation's own intelligence services. He's given aide, comfort, and praise to murderous regimes in Russia, North Korea, and the Philippines. Meanwhile, he upbraided our NATO allies like a sleazy collection's agent. He also issued long, public criticisms of China as a currency manipulator only to reverse himself after a ten-minute chat with China's President Xi.

In March of 2018, Trump remarked of Xi, "He's now president for life. President for life. No, he's great. And look, he was able to do that. I think it's great. Maybe we'll have to give that a shot someday."

Trump remains unapologetic for such an inappropriate "joke" as China deepens its disrespect for human rights.

After the Obama Administration saw a weakening of America's position in the world, conservatives hoped for a Republican President who would re-assert strong American leadership. While Trump's supporters convince each other that he is what they had hoped for, the reality is, he has left world leaders who support freedom wondering where America stands anymore.

The GOP's position on traditional values had stood firm despite some sex scandals over the years. Some hypocritically aped ideas of "family values" while violating their marriage vows with adultery, but the charlatans found themselves pushed out when exposed.

Today, the Republican Party's family values have taken a beating under President Trump. Family values leaders know about his lifetime of adultery, philandering, cheating business partners, bullying, and being abusive—and they support President Trump anyway.

Tony Perkins of the Family Research Council put it this way to Politco's Off Message podcast, "We kind of gave him—'All right, you get a mulligan. You get a do-over here.'"

Why do they tolerate his disgraceful behavior in office? Simple, Trump has bought them with promised appointments to the judicial and executive branch offices and promises to pass favorable laws. Yet the success of cultural conservatism doesn't lie in mere political victories. A key to long-term success is moral authority. They've traded long-term credibility for short-term political wins. Like Esau, they've traded their birthright for a bowl of stew.

One doesn't have to side with social conservatives in the culture war to be alarmed by the ethical failures of the Trump White House.

The White House has a whole web of conflict of interests, not the least of which involve the President, his daughter, and his son-in-law (both are his advisors.) The machinations and utterly unpleasant personalities has created a toxic environment few people want to work in, leaving countless government posts unfilled, with incredible, unprecedented turnover.

So much more could be said about the indictments, the scandals, and the misconduct of many White House officials but detailing all that's wrong with the Trump White House would take too much space.

Further, I'd have to constantly print new editions of this book to update an all-inclusive list. However, the public is sure to remember the dysfunction and lack of integrity of these years. Should they ever forget, Democrats will be glad to remind them that most Republicans either stood by silently or outright excused Trump.

The Republican's defenses of this weak administration will be a burden they'll carry for years to come. Even more severe than the burden Republicans had to deal with in the wake of Watergate for their defense of Nixon.

Some in the GOP will assert not every Republican drank the Trump Kool-Aid and they personally didn't vote for Trump. Some in a post-Trump GOP will claim they privately disagreed with him and he's not representative of what they will be. However, this talk will alienate Trump diehards, who will continue to buy into his strong-man image and deny the reality of his weak, corrupt administration long after it. If you get into a room with some elderly Republicans, criticizing Nixon can still be a problem.

The damage Trump's done to the Republican brand is so severe, we need a conservative party that will unite as one to repudiate the Trump era's wrongs. That won't happen in the GOP.

Chapter 2
The Good Will Deficit:
They're Not Listening

When I ran for the Idaho House in 2004, I walked across my legislative district going door to door. I had encounters where I introduced myself to voters and got asked a simple question, "Are you a Republican?"

If I answered yes, I was sent on my way. They had no interest in what I had to say when I bore the "Republican" label. Doubtless many more politely gave me a moment but didn't consider what I had to say for the same reasons.

A Democrat running for office faces a similar bias from different people. This is a fact of human existence. Most decide to screen out people who come presenting to them. If we didn't, we'd waste countless hours talking on our front porches to politicians and controversial religious groups or listening to long pitches from telemarketers about amazing opportunities.

This simple reality is lost on much of the Right. Conservatives can spend hours honing arguments. Many believe if you can come up with a watertight, logical argument, it will persuade people. What many don't understand that it doesn't matter how good your arguments are. These days, people often are only interested in hearing arguments that validate their own beliefs.

Further, many people won't listen to Republicans because many believe Republicans don't care about them or are ought right hostile. Some of this is the result of media bias and existing cultural bias. Some of it is Republicans' own fault.

First, the media bias needs to be acknowledged. Not every story Donald Trump dislikes is "fake news," but media bias is real. I don't think members of the media want to report fake stories. Most want to give you a false impression without speaking a false word.

News media bias shows up in both subtle and obvious ways. First is how racially offensive statements. Imagine if a Trump had said, "In Delaware, the largest growth of population is Indian Americans, moving from India. You cannot go to a 7-11 or a Dunkin' Donuts unless you have a slight Indian accent. I'm not joking."

The stereotype of Indians working at convenience stores would be condemned as yet another sign of Trump's racism. Any Republican politician would never be able to get away from the statement. Yet, that quote is real and actually from former Vice-President Joe Biden. He explained it once and the media forgave it and forgot it. It's only mentioned when listing Biden's gaffes, something the media avoids doing while Biden is on the ballot. Biden is seen as a comical fellow who stumbles in his words but is no racist.

Were a Republican to make that statement, he or she would never live it down. If they delivered an apology, it would be parsed endlessly and explained why it was insufficient and why their original statement showed what he or she truly believed. We would be told this moment revealed what type of person they really were.

Another difference is how Biden's gaffes affect his overall image. While the media can have fun with Biden's gaffes, it doesn't treat them as the totality of the man. They treat him as more than just the sum of his gaffes, but as a politician who has skills such as being able to communicate to and relate with the working people of this country. They present his goofy gaffes as part of his charm.

A gaffe-prone Vice-President of an earlier generation, Republican Dan Quayle, was turned into a joke and treated as little more than a gaffe machine. In truth, he too was a skilled politician who defeated long-term Democratic incumbents to win elections to the House in 1976 and the Senate in 1980. He won re-election in the Democratic wave year of 1986 by 22 points while other Freshman Republicans elected to the Senate in 1980 were dropping like flies. We were led to believe Quayle achieved this by being a complete idiot.

Also, the way both good and bad deeds of politicians are reported says a lot. For example, many think of Biden as a likable, kind, generous guy and peg Mitt Romney as a heartless, greedy businessman. When it comes to personal giving, Biden is the stingy one compared to Romney. ABC News reported, in the decade before Biden's 2008 Vice-President run, he and his wife, a college instructor, gave an average of $369 per year to charity, only 0.3% of their annual income. How much did Romney give? His 2011 tax return revealed he gave to charity 29.0% of his substantial annual income.

George W. Bush was pilloried and ruthlessly vilified by the media. Kanye West declared, "George Bush doesn't care about Black people."

Another pop star told a different story on Instagram. The Irish U2 Bono captioned a picture of President Bush and him together saying, "More than eleven million [Africans] are alive thanks to this man's creation of PEPFAR." (President's Emergency Plan for AIDS Relief.) PEPFAR is a program to help Africans diagnosed with HIV/AIDS that has been an unmitigated success.

Had PEPFAR been created by Obama, we would never hear the end of it. It would play into the media's messianic narrative about Obama. Because it is Bush, the work of PEPFAR is little acknowledged and even less credit goes to the man who created it. Far more remember Kayne West's unfair slur.

Compare the media's buzz around Barack Obama in 2008 to the media's treatment of Marco Rubio in 2016. Both were well-polished speakers from humble minority communities. Both were also charismatic and connected with voters beyond the typical politics of race. With Obama, the media glossed over troubling details in Obama's past such as his holding a fundraiser at the home of a terrorist bomb-planter from the Weather Underground.

The mainstream media didn't focus on Rubio's inspirational narrative or what his election would mean for young Latinos. The media did see Rubio's potential. He ran ten or more points better against the eventual Democratic nominee than Trump in trial runs, and his statewide showing in Florida had indicated he could make inroads in traditionally Democratic constituencies.

The New York Times as a New York paper was uniquely positioned to expose to the nation the troubling aspects of Donald Trump's business record. Instead, in June 2015, they ran an expose on the fact Senator Rubio had had four traffic tickets in the previous eighteen years, while his wife had thirteen. Meanwhile, Trump had been involved in hundreds of lawsuits which didn't trouble the New York Times until Trump clinched the nomination.

Members of the media are often eager to do their own side a solid favor. During the coverage of the Monica Lewinsky scandal and President Clinton's impeachment for perjury before a federal grand jury and obstruction of justice, the media echoed the line it was all about a backwards puritanical view of sex that baffled the rest of the civilized world. CNN even featured a report with a German man complaining we were acting like our "pilgrim fathers."

In the wake of #MeToo, the media and the left have backed away from this support of Clinton as they go after President Trump over allegations of sexual misconduct. They've realized it undermines their credibility. As Miss Lewinsky said in a Vanity Fair piece, she's now seen there was a "problematic" question of consent in a relationship between the most powerful man on the face of the Earth and a twenty-one-year-old intern young enough to be his daughter. Conservatives argued this twenty years ago, but it was brushed aside.

The media's ultimate act of defending Clinton came from CBS News. They'd determined Juanita Broderick made an allegation of rape against the President of the United States that was so credible, they gave her full interview on the premiere TV news magazine *60 Minutes,* but they ensured it didn't air until Clinton had been acquitted in his Senate Impeachment trial.

Media bias isn't limited to the news. The entertainment media plays a key role. It helps shape attitudes towards various groups, and it shows a clear bias in who its villains are. Often, they are Republicans or symbols of conservative values: business executives, ministers, religious people, and members of the military. Broad archetypes get splashed across the TV screen. The bigoted Archie Bunker and the clueless yuppie Alex Keaton define conservatives. The only truly good conservative you'll ever see on television or film is one that's slightly misguided and on a journey to achieving a liberal's blissful wokeness.

The entertainment industry's biases have become more obvious over the years as the Oscars became populated by well-made left-wing propaganda, but they've been in media of all sorts for decades in the most unexpected places.

Take Bill Cosby's comedy *Ghost Dad*, where he portrayed a dead insurance salesman who was haunting his family and trying to fake his way through a life insurance examination. His nerdy, annoying fourteen-year-old black neighbor, Stuart, ended up finding out something was wrong with Cosby's character and trying to blackmail him. Though the movie had nothing to do with politics, the character announces he's a Republican.

In the midst of an unfunny comedy, the writer decided to make Stuart his picture of what Republicans are, and Black Republicans in particular, for no reason other than he could. I don't suggest *Ghost Dad* alone changed anyone's mind about Republicans, but enough moments like this in media occur to shape the minds of the unwary.

The Republicans' chances of making political conversions have depended on fair-minded individuals who could face an onslaught of media that portrays Republicans as crazy jingoists, hypocrites, and abusive towards women and minorities and conclude, *Republicans can't possibly all be like the comic book villains.*

Of course, this was before Trump.

Ways Republicans Hurt Themselves Before Trump

Having acknowledged the powerful role of media bias, we have to say that the Republicans have a greater enemy than the media: themselves.

For example, Republicans have made several mistakes on the issues of race. Republicans bristle at charges of racism, saying they don't hate minorities. They wouldn't refuse service to a black person. They're not opposed to black people holding any job. They won't reject a candidate because of their race. Most white conservatives won't object if their children marry minorities.

White conservatives associate racism with history's violent racists like Hitler and the Ku Klux Klan. However, "we're not racist, we just hate political correctness" is used as a license to say stupid, insensitive, and racially divisive things. You can be against illegal immigration and not anti-Hispanic. You can be against racial preferences and set asides as reverse discrimination without being anti-minority. You wouldn't know it, though, listening to the folks who don't even try to state their views in ways that don't inflame racial strife.

It's possible to be "not racist" and to also be disrespectful, ignorant, and uncaring toward minorities. However, the latter is racism in the eyes of many minorities. Republicans are not being fair or wise to expect minorities to read their hearts and see their intentions are "not racist."

The biggest issue for many minorities, particularly Blacks, may be how the Republicans have opposed President Obama. To be clear, President Obama fully deserved to be opposed. During his eight years in office, there's little that he did which I agree with. However, the opposition should have stuck to the issues and it often didn't, especially on social media.

During the Obama years, Republican attacks on Obama often crossed a line. There were insults on Mrs. Obama's appearance and the allegation she lacked class, with unflattering still photos shared around the world. Images of Obama donning Somali garb during a visit to Somalia and the suggestion he was a "Secret Muslim" were shared frequently on Facebook.

The worst of this was the birthers, in particular the conspiracy theorists. President Obama was born in Hawaii, but these theorists insist he was born abroad in Indonesia or perhaps in Kenya (where his father hailed from.) The sort of massive conspiracy that this required was impossible and no proof of such a conspiracy exists.

Rather, the conspiracy theory birthers argued that this happened and their chief piece of evidence was Obama had not released his full long-form birth certificate. I viewed the issue as a distraction. When I became a Republican and got involved in politics, I didn't sign up for foolishness. At the time, I blamed Obama (everything was Obama's fault then.) He could solve everything by just producing the long-form birth certificate.

Looking back, I can understand why he delayed. No other President was asked to produce this sort of documentation. While many people believed Obama wasn't born in the USA, no one had good reason to. If *The National Enquirer* had published a story stating Obama was a space alien, should he have been expected to give a DNA sample to prove his humanity?

Plus Obama wasn't required to stop his opponents from making fools of themselves, and that's why I wanted him to produce it. It wasn't until Donald Trump took up the birther cause as his own that Obama produced the form. And the conspiracy theorists started the inevitable "it's a forgery" argument rather than concede they were wrong.

What I call a "constitutional birtherism" became more prominent. The argument doesn't depend on Obama being born in some exotic locale. Rather, it argues when the Constitution requires a President be "a natural born citizen" that this required both parents to be U.S. Citizens in the eighteenth century.

Most legal scholars would point out the Fourteenth Amendment declares anyone born in the United States or a subject of its jurisdiction U.S. citizens, which overrules the question of what "natural born citizen" originally meant. Not everyone agrees. According to University of Delaware law Professor Mary Brigid McManamon, the fourteenth Amendment "naturalizes at birth" those who are not natural born citizens by the eighteenth-century definition.

This is a novel theory, but this is a question for the courts. The courts are never going to use a highly debatable legal theory to disqualify a sitting U.S. President. As such, all the time, energy, and bandwidth spent pushing this was a complete waste of time, money, and credibility.

Most conservative leaders stayed away from the birtherism issue. They weren't going to demand a birth certificate. They knew the theory was rubbish. However, they also weren't going to try and disabuse people at the grassroots of this notion less they be labeled a RINO.

What minorities saw in the Obama years were Republicans seeking in the most desperate, absurd ways to de-legitimize America's first Black President. To be sure, some unfairly equated mere opposition to Obama's policies with racism. Nonetheless, the Republicans who spent eight years trying to degrade and delegitimize the first Black man to the White House did great damage to the Republican cause.

Beyond the reaction to Obama and poorly-framed arguments on racially charged issues such as immigration and affirmative action, on the whole, the Republican Party didn't practice the politics of racial antagonism. Those who did generally didn't make it far in national politics.

In addition, some in the GOP fought hard to reach minorities and to promote conservative women. Strong, female conservative leaders rebutted the Democrats' accusation the GOP was waging a "war on women."

Former Congressman and 1996 Presidential Candidate Jack Kemp has offered some conservative solutions to the problems in minority communities. Conservative leaders such as President George W. Bush actively reached out to minority communities. The Republican National Committee acknowledged the party's problem with winning the minority vote and pledged to address this after reviewing its "autopsy" of why it lost the 2012 Presidential election.

Despite the efforts of good people to broaden the GOP base, largely the party remained indifferent to minorities. The Republican Party has won many elections on the strength of the white vote while getting wiped out among minorities. Most minorities live in districts and states the GOP has written off as unwinnable in fact.

Rather than try to understand the problems minorities face, come up with conservative solutions, and do the hard work of persuading minorities to their side, Republicans opted to ignore the problem and focus on winning the easiest to get votes.

However, minorities often view such indifference as disrespectful, even the equal of the active racial contempt that constitutes racism in Conservatives' understanding. Republicans did at least generally avoid engaging white identity politics—until Trump came along.

Chapter 3
Trump's Effect

The GOP already had problems with race relations, but Trump has made them beyond repair. To detail every incident would take far too long. Trump's history of racial discrimination goes back to when the Nixon Administration sued Trump's company for discriminating against Black renters. I'll focus on events of the 2016 presidential campaign and the Trump administration for the sake of time.

Trump's Twitter account is powerful. He has repeatedly used it to share posts from white Supremacists who argue there is a coordinated attempt to eliminate "the white race." Fortune's Ben Kharakh quoted Andrew Anglin of the racist Daily Stormer website as saying, "Trump is giving us the old wink-wink." He took heart in the fact that Trump retweeted two "White Genocide" posts within a minute.

"Whereas the odd White genocide tweet could be a random occurrence, it isn't statistically possible that two of them back to back could be a random occurrence. It could only be deliberate…Today in America the air is cold and it tastes like victory."

With such positive feelings from the racist community, it was no wonder when the Ku Klux Klan endorsed Trump. In 1984, the Klan endorsed Ronald Reagan and he disavowed them. As for Trump, he didn't disavow the Klan's endorsement and only attacked racism after he won the Presidency. Even then, he attacked it with far less ferocity than he had attacked Ted Cruz.

Trump during his campaign insisted the Central Park Five, five black teens who were accused of raping a white woman, were guilty. The fact DNA evidence had cleared them fourteen years previously didn't faze him.

President Trump responded to the lawsuit against Trump University by attacking Judge Gonzalo Curiel as a "Mexican judge" biased against him since Trump wanted to build the wall.

Judge Curiel is an American judge born in Indiana and confirmed by the United States Senate. While his parents were from Mexico, Curiel has shown no bias against Trump. He could have scheduled the Trump University trial to occur during the election, rather than more than a week after it. In early 2018, Judge Curiel issued a ruling that allowed the Trump administration to go ahead with construction of a border wall. Trump's ignorant attacks on Curiel were utterly false.

In Charlottesville in August 2017, white supremacists planned a "Unite the Right" rally and they clashed with protesters. A white supremacist rammed his car into the protesters, striking twenty people and killing thirty-two-year-old Heather Heyer.

The President should have unequivocally denounced the racists. Instead, he insisted there were "good people on both sides." Never mind that only one of those sides had caused a fatality and was headed by the vile alt-right activist Richard Spencer and marched beneath the evil banner of the Nazi Party.

For some Trump supporters, it was too much. Black Republican political analyst Gianno Caldwell went on Fox and Friends and denounced Trump. A tearful Caldwell confessed he hadn't slept the night before because Trump "had betrayed the conscience of the nation."

Caldwell went on to say, "He's failed us, and it's very unfortunate that our president would say things like he did in that press conference yesterday when he says, 'There are good people on the side of the Nazis. They weren't all Nazis and they weren't all white supremacists.' Mr. President, good people don't pal around with Nazis and white supremacists."

On top of Trump's history of at least encouraging racists, his treatment of women is also repugnant. Again, the full list of incidents is too lengthy to go through, so I will highlight a few incidents that illustrate the President's general disrespect for women.

He mocked fellow 2016 President Candidate Carly Fiorina's appearance, saying, "Look at that face! Would anyone vote for that? Can you imagine that, the face of our next president?!'

Trump took exception to Megyn Kelly's tough questioning of him in an August 2015 debate and said, "You could see there was blood coming out of her eyes, blood coming out of her wherever." That last part was widely seen as a reference to Ms. Kelly's menstrual cycle. Trump later claimed he meant her nose by "wherever," but this remains disrespectful and ill-considered.

The most alarming of Trump's statements on women came during the 2016 campaign when a 2009 tape showed him bragging to Billy Bush about how he could assault women at will. "And when you're a star, they let you do it. You can do anything." According to Trump, that included grabbing women by the genitals.

At least twenty former *Apprentice* employees have accused Trump of lewd conduct. More than a dozen women have accused Trump of sexual assault and harassment throughout his life.

Also, Trump inspires Republicans to attack victims who come forward as false accusers without proof of this serious crime. Take the case of Alabama Senate candidate Roy Moore, who faced credible charges of sexual misconduct with minors. Breitbart News strained to undermine the credibility of Moore's victims. After the election, Breitbart Editor Alex Marlow admitted he believed the victims' testimony and cast aspersions because, "It's about what's coming next for President Trump."

Marlow and the Breitbart organization and many less candid Republican sources have sought to undermine the credibility of all victims of sexual assault in order to protect Trump.

Trump's staff secretary, Rob Porter, was credibly accused of assault by two of his ex-wives. One victim produced photographic evidence of Porter's abuse. This led to the FBI denying Porter security clearance. Trump responded by wishing Porter well and complaining on Twitter, "Is there no longer any such thing as due process?" Keep in mind this is the same Trump who alleged the Central Park Five were guilty after they'd been cleared by DNA evidence and a couple weeks later would call for taking guns without due process.

In the era of "#metoo" we need to be aware not all victims are female and not all predators are male. Further, predators have been known to make false accusations in order to incite others to punish their victims for them. For this reason, it is vital that we carefully examine a testimony's credibility before we punish someone. Even feminists acknowledge the potential for overreach. Yet, Trump is not a credible person to raise this issue, since his reasons for doing so are clearly self-serving.

Trump wants to ensure the charges against him are never believed, so he casts doubt on anyone who testifies they have been harassed. There's hardly been a sexual assault case where he hasn't sided with the man and attacked the woman, no matter how much evidence backs her testimony.

He defended Mike Tyson when the heavyweight boxer was convicted of rape. He defended Bill Clinton in the 1990s, only to turn on him and label Hillary an enabler during his 2016 presidential campaign. He defended former Fox News host Bill O'Reilly though O'Reilly agreed to a $32 million settlement in a harassment case. So he defended Moore despite the existence of multiple credible reports. He defended Porter despite physical evidence of attacks.

The primary exception is the Central Park Five. This may lead the casual observer to conclude the only men that Trump believes commit sex crimes are minorities who aren't celebrities. It should be noted, even in that case, Trump couldn't be said to have believed the woman as she was rendered unconscious and had no memory of what happened.

As I heard one person observe, to Donald Trump, there is nothing more credible than a man's denial. Trump's position and the fact most Republicans are looking the other way is a death knell to the party among young women.

Republicans have been convinced en masse that Democrats have run out of real victims to bring forward against Republicans, that the women brought forward now are all liars. A CNN poll from December showed only 18% of Republicans believed the allegations against Trump.

In addition, some conservatives fume about the vulgar name of the pink cat ears hats worn at the Women's Marches and complain about the protestors using the same vulgarity on signs. The same conservatives rarely acknowledge why those hats are worn and those signs are carried. Trump used that vulgarity when he bragged about molesting women. If you are more bothered by what protestors call their headgear than you are by a powerful man boasting that he is entitled to grab women's genitals, please re-examine your values and the priority you give them.

Donald Trump will be the gift that keeps on giving to far left feminist groups. They have been able to get many women involved in their groups who had no interest in many of their radical pet causes. New York Times columnist David Brook has said that Millennials do not "see abortion as integral to their feminism." However, not being assaulted or abused is integral.

Many conservative women have sought to reclaim the feminism label to stand for empowering women to live up to their full potential. They reject the liberal feminist mentality which turns women into helpless victims who need the government to provide for them. Spending four to eight years supporting Trump will destroy the conservative feminists' credibility.

There's also a generation gap. Trump won on the strength of voters 45 and older, losing younger voters by a decisive margin. It's easy to imagine this is because young liberals will grow older and become more conservative. To a degree, this may be true.

However, a generation gap also exists among younger Evangelicals. We have not abandoned the conservative convictions of the generation of Russell Moore of the Southern Baptist Church Ethics and Religious Commission. He opposed Trump and pointed to resolutions on the importance of character that the Southern Baptist Convention passed when a Democrat with character flaws was in the White House while his colleagues ignore Trump's flaws.

The generation gap over Trump is different than in years past. Younger generations are more aware of bullying and abuse and are firmly against such.

The President of the United States is the world's most powerful cyber bully. The party that champions him will have trouble ever winning the upcoming generation.

Trump supporters will mock xennials[1] and millennials as "snowflakes" for our viewing Trump as a despicable bully rather than as an admirable strong man. Mocking the xennials and millennials is not a wise long-term political strategy. Analysts estimate we will make up 40% of voters in the 2020 election and even more in elections to come. Donald Trump's 2016 coalition is not a sustainable winning coalition. It depends on white voters of dying generations.

In 2020, the xennials will be thirty-seven to forty-three years old. The millennials will be twenty-four to thirty-six years old, and the electorate will be more ethnically diverse.

Beyond demographics, the party faces a crisis of personnel. A party isn't made up of the people who check the party name on the registration box. It's the activists that define the heart, soul, and guts of the party. Many Republican activists have resigned rather than support Trump. This included high-ranking officials in the Federation of Republican Women, College Republicans, and state and county Republican Parties, as well as people who had been elected as delegates to the National Convention or the Electoral College.

Within the Trump bubble, such defections are deemed to be traitors or members of "the establishment" (whatever that means.) Yet, the truth is those who have dropped out of the party cut across a wide ideological swath from a tea party state Vice Chair in Michigan to more moderate Republicans like a Texas GOP elector who voted for John Kasich rather than Trump in the 2016 electoral college. For them all, it comes to an issue of conscience.

Many of these people are young and talented, who would have had much to offer the party and had accomplished much. Mindy Finn, Evan McMullin's running mate in 2016, is a thirty-something pro-life Jewish conservative and digital strategist for the Republican Party. McMullin, with his decade of service overseas, was the chief policy strategist for the House Republicans. They both had the profiles of people who could be key leaders for the future of the GOP. Now that's lost thanks to Trump.

Some who stayed in the Party and continued to work for its change have had enough. Take the case of Kyle McDaniel, a twenty-eight-year-old Virginian elected to his state's Central Committee. McDaniel had a promising future in the GOP. He bided his time, while dealing with stupid and racially insensitive comments within the Virginia GOP. Trump finally pushed things too far with comments denigrating Haitians and others who come from the Third World.

---

[1] Xennials were born between 1977 and 1983, on the cusp of Gen X and the millennials, and enjoyed a Gen X childhood before modern tech first emerged in the mid-1990s.

McDaniel announced his resignation from the Central Committee and from the GOP, saying, "The President's unnecessary and appalling comments regarding the Haitian people, and the defense of those comments by party leaders, are the straw that broke the camel's back. I have been to Haiti's slums, twice, and worked alongside those who have to call it home; my wife and I are considering adopting a Haitian child. There is no rationalization of the President's comments that makes them anything other than what they are: a claim that Haitians do not deserve a chance to be American."

Beyond the demographics and lost talent issues is the issue many leaders parted company with the GOP over: conscience and personal integrity. The message from the party leadership has been that people of conscience are not welcomed. As for personal integrity, the Trump administration has made it clear you have to be willing to sacrifice that in the modern GOP.

A person with integrity may still believe Trump's GOP represents the best of two bad options, but the actions in the party within the past year would at minimum make us think hard about giving our time and energy to the party. So who will take jobs with the GOP? Who will volunteer hours and work to organize precincts and run county parties?

The short answer is people who don't care about integrity, honesty or decency: the people fanatical in their adoration of the President, sycophants, toadies, and people whose top priority is their own personal advancement.

The logic of the Trump-era GOP welcomes people without integrity. After all, the new party motto ought to be, "Just win, baby." People without ethics make for effective operatives—until they get caught in more scandals, resulting in more problems and a further loss of faith by the American public.

Many conservatives will choose to sit out the next four-to-eight years, let Trumpism run its course, and hope to then rebuild from the rubble. What will such conservatives inherit if they retake the GOP? A party whose reputation is irreparably damaged by Trump, a feckless GOP congress, and the unethical people working in the Trump Administration. Whom will Trump attract to party leadership? How long will it take the GOP to recover from Trump?

For a historical example, consider the Catholic vote.

There was a great deal of anti-Catholic sentiment in the GOP of the late nineteenth century and early twentieth century. That image was personified in an 1884 rally for Republican Presidential candidate James Blaine.

Rev. Dr. Samuel Burchard said, "We are Republicans, and don't propose to leave our party and identify ourselves with the party whose antecedents have been rum, Romanism, and rebellion."

This anti-Catholic statement was key to Democrat Grover Cleveland's win that year as the Democrats turned out the Irish Catholics in New York. The antipathy towards the GOP among Catholics continued with Catholics being a key Democratic voting block for years.

Only when the GOP nominated a candidate as good as Eisenhower or the Democrats nominated someone as bad as George McGovern would the Catholic vote be in question. It took Ronald Reagan to consistently make the Catholic vote competitive again. Even then, the Catholics continued to vote more Democratic than the general population until George W. Bush, 116 years after Reverend Burchard's statement on rum, Romanism, and rebellion.

Based on this, I don't believe the Republicans will recover with the key voter groups that Trump has alienated during my lifetime.

Many advantages do come with the GOP's ballot access, war chest, and organization. It's easy to understand why some might choose to wait out the Trump years in the hopes of changing it. However, even if you could, the GOP's brand and credibility has been utterly destroyed. So much so, the more effective strategy for advancing conservative values is to start a new part.

Chapter 4
Primary Truth

President Trump once declared, regarding the Republican Primary, "The system is rigged." He got that correct, but he got the reasons wrong. Still, his opponents within the GOP need to grasp that reality, or they're going to waste a lot of time, money, and energy that could be better spent.

Some dream of a primary challenge unseating President Trump in 2020. This is not going to happen. President Trump is running again, and he will be our nominee again.

Trump will not attract a solid primary challenger. It would be a political suicide mission. There are several reasons for this.

First, primary challenges to incumbent Presidents often hand the election to the other party. In 1968, Eugene McCarthy ran against incumbent President Lyndon B. Johnson, forcing Johnson out, and the Democrats lost the White House. In 1976, Ronald Reagan challenged President Gerald Ford and Ford lost to Jimmy Carter. In 1980, Edward Kennedy ran against President Carter and Carter lost. In 1992, Pat Buchanan challenged President George H.W. Bush and Republicans lost the White House. In contrast, in 1984, 1996, 2004, and 2012, the incumbents didn't face a primary challenge and won re-election.

A challenger to the President would lose and become the scapegoat for the party's losses. Due to the party's bad feelings, the challenger would never actually be nominated for President.

Second, as the President, Trump controls the RNC and the rules for the Republican Presidential nominating process, which in itself is a discouragement to challengers. We'll discuss this in more detail later. If the danger to

Trump's re-election becomes apparent, changes would be made by the RNC to make it even harder for a challenger to compete against him.

Third, primaries tend to draw partisan Republicans. Such are now trained to either deny or ignore the President's flaws and are going to be difficult to convince to change direction.

Finally, the President would never endorse any person who defeated him, nor will Trump's worshipful base. To the contrary, the President would seek revenge against whoever ousted him. As such, the highest prize a Republican Primary challenger to Trump would get is having the TV networks include the tag "Former Republican Presidential Nominee" under their name on Cable News appearances. They would never be elected President.

What if President Trump doesn't run? That hope once was reasonable, given the President's age and his scandals, but he's already announced for re-election. If a health problem did force him to drop out, we'd have the same flawed nominating system that gave us Trump in the first place. This system harms our ability to get good candidates nominated.

The system that has elevated President Trump gave us many previous Republican nominees. This is not a criticism of these men. As the saying goes, "Hate the game, not the player."

The Republican nominating contest begins the spring of the year before the election with candidates establishing campaigns in Iowa, New Hampshire, and South Carolina. While votes are taken directly for the candidates in most contests, most delegates elected to the convention are bound to the candidates for those first few ballots.

The primary season kicks off with the Iowa Caucus and is followed by the New Hampshire and South Carolina Primaries and the Nevada Caucus in February. While some unsuccessful campaigns leave the field of battle, many campaigns with no chance of winning continue to crowd the race, take up time on the debate stage, and split the vote.

In 2016, Ben Carson never finished higher than fourth in the first four contests and John Kasich's second place finish in New Hampshire was his only good performance, with him finishing in single digits in every other state. Carson continued through Super Tuesday and Kasich stayed in through May.

March brings Super Tuesday, in which eleven states voted in 2016. This is lower than in past years. The 2008 contest featured twenty-four states voting on Super Tuesday. However, in 2016, twenty-six states plus several U.S. Territories voted during the entire month of March, with elections being held on nearly every Tuesday and on multiple weekends also.

After that, early April is a dead zone with only Wisconsin holding a vote. The action picks up towards the third Tuesday of the month with New York voting, followed by several North Eastern states in the Acela Corridor at the end of April. The remaining states vote in May and June. In 2016, Indiana was the only state to hold a meaningful contest that late. When all the others voted, Trump had already clinched the nomination.

These states' votes becoming perfunctory does not concern the RNC. Since 1988, the focus of the GOP nominating contest has been on reaching a fast conclusion, not on reaching a good conclusion. The thought behind this is, the quicker the nominating process is resolved and the party unites, the sooner preparation can be made for the fall elections, and the more victory is assured. This is not always true. In 2008, John McCain clinched the Republican nomination in early March while the contest for the Democratic nomination continued until the Convention in August.

In the fall, Obama won the popular vote by seven percentage points and the most Electoral of any Presidential Candidate since 1996.

This system has several major flaws that prevent a good candidate from winning.

The first problem is inherent, the role momentum plays. Winning in early states bolsters a candidate's standing. The media conversation becomes, "Can this candidate be stopped?" This is quickly added to by media discussion of delegate math. A candidate who has won early states and done well on Super Tuesday has a better chance of winning the nomination outright. This is what the political analysts talk about and the campaign surrogates' debate, with the push of the coverage being how undefeatable the frontrunner is.

Should momentum play a role in Presidential primaries? It doesn't in the general election. Kentucky and Indiana's polls close an hour before anyone else's. Their results don't influence the votes of the rest of the states. Imagine if two states closed their polls months before everyone else and voters spent the] general election campaign hearing media coverage about how Candidate X's victory in those two states now requires Candidate Y to win 60% of all outstanding electoral votes to "rob" Candidate X of the presidency.

Frontloading the primary, with the majority of states voting early, creates massive pressure on voters in the remaining states to support the frontrunner whether they want to or not.

 Momentum is far less important in a non-frontloaded system. In 1976, Ronald Reagan lost the first six nominating contests but won the seventh and did well the rest of the way through, nearly defeating Gerald Ford. In that year, the Iowa Caucuses had been on January 19th with the New Hampshire primary a month later on February 24th, with a grand total of five states voting in the month of March followed by two voting in the month of April.

The push to back the frontrunner is aided by winner-takes-all primaries. Most early Republican Primaries, and all Democratic Primaries, are based on proportional allocation by state or congressional district, or some-times both.

With the Democrats, it's consistent throughout the process. With the Republicans, it varies from state to state. This leads to inequities in how delegates are allocated. In 2006 in South Carolina, Trump won 32% of the vote in the state's primary and won all 50 delegates. In Texas, Ted Cruz won 44% of the vote and received only 104 of the state's 155 delegates.

When most states, even the truly late states, proportionally allocate their delegates, a frontrunner's winner-takes-all victories distort the process and lead to a "delegate math" calculation that renders the rest of the country irrelevant.

The nature of the primary system can mean late-voting states get stuck with candidates ill-suited to them. This happened in 2016 when Ted Cruz remained the last serious challenger to Trump. John Kasich had little money left and had only won his home state. Trump won all six states that voted on the last two primary dates in April, with Cruz finishing *third* in all but one.

While Cruz was perfectly suited to winning in Iowa, Texas, Idaho, and Utah, he was such a poor fit for these later East Coast states, Trump crushed him there and finished him off in Indiana. The stronger showing by Kasich suggested a center-right candidate who had a shot of winning could have given Trump a more serious challenge. The citizens of these late-voting states didn't get to vote for a candidate that suited them, and this helped the frontrunner.

Who ends up the frontrunner? The Iowa Caucuses and New Hampshire primary serve to create a situation where the election for President is a free-for-all. This allows a candidate to run a grassroots campaign on a small budget and become a Presidential frontrunner.

This happened in 1976 when Jimmy Carter went from an obscure one-term former Governor of Georgia to the 39th President of the United States based on his campaign in the early states. This could be seen in 2000 when John McCain won a landslide based on his more than 100 town halls in the state of New Hampshire. In 2012 Rick Santorum won the Iowa Caucuses with a miniscule budget by visiting every county in the State of Iowa.

However, while Iowa and New Hampshire are built to give a shot to a grassroots candidate, the rest of the calendar is built to crush the upstart. Frontloading became a thing in the 1988 election cycle and it has helped front-runners like the Bushes to claim the nomination quickly.

Politics has traditionally been all about organization. In 1976, candidates only had to worry about nine states voting between January and the April, which meant funds, organizations, and ballot access in later states could be taken care of over time. Under the front-loaded system, campaigns have to be concerned about ballot access in every state in the Union.

Low budget campaigns that focused on a breakthrough in Iowa or New Hampshire often rely on volunteers to get their name on the ballot, but also have to find funds to pay filing fees. Candidates like Mike Huckabee, Rand

Paul, and Carly Fiorina got eliminated within the first couple of primaries but their names appeared on ballots across the country.

In some cases, a legitimate candidate may not make the ballot. When Virginians went to the polls in 2012, they had a choice between Mitt Romney and Ron Paul. Neither of Romney's principle opponents, Rick Santorum and Newt Gingrich, were able to make the state's onerous ballot requirements. The result was Romney winning every delegate in the state.

The candidates backed by the political establishment could count on party regulars to back them. The rest of conservatives often watch from a distance. Why invest time, energy, and money into Candidate X if they may not make it past the early primaries? This was the case for me in 2012, when I could have supported several conservative candidates but I waited until after the Iowa Caucuses to see who would emerge. I then endorsed Rick Santorum and found myself invited to join the campaign as state coordinator—less than six weeks before my state's caucus.

Well-run campaigns don't worry about this. In 2000, I attended a Lincoln Day Dinner in Montana where a couple from Wisconsin were there to gather 500 signatures to get Governor George W. Bush on Montana's primary ballot. I was collecting signatures for Alan Keyes. I reflected that it was curious the Bush campaign paid to send people from the Midwest to gather signatures while Keyes had relied upon a local nineteen-year-old volunteer.

The system has been designed for the party establishment to win, but the power of organization is not absolute in the Information Age. Media coverage and the amount of press received can vault a candidate to frontrunner status. This is what happened with John McCain in 2008. He was a beloved hero of the media for his maverick status. He was not well-liked at all by party leaders for the many times he opposed the Bush Administration.

However, positive media coverage drove the process and attracted many Independents, particularly in the open primary states of South Carolina and New Hampshire. Media coverage drove him to victory in those early primaries and momentum carried him the rest of the way.

This was nothing compared to the treatment the media gave Trump. The media covered Trump's rallies and speeches without interruption, which was unprecedented. Trump dominated the media coverage. The analytics company mediaQuant reported Trump received $5 billion in media coverage during the entirety of the campaign. In the latter portion of the campaign, Marco Rubio stooped to Trump's level and began his rallies with insults designed to rankle Trump. This got media coverage, however, the media cut away when Rubio moved to discussing policies.

The media's coverage ignored problems in Trump's record such as his fraudulent Trump University until after he'd gotten the nomination. Before October, the media withheld the *Access Hollywood* tapes featuring Trump's now-famous bragging about sexual assault. They sat on stories of Trump abusing his authority as a pageant owner to walk in on naked young women. It's not unreasonable to conclude that the media had decided to pump Trump up with positive media coverage in the primaries only to spring October surprises on him to throw the election to the Democrats. It failed because the Democrats nominated Hilary Clinton, whose ethical flaws equal Trump's and voters perceived the businessman as less corrupt than the former first lady.

The current Republican Primary process guarantees the nominee will be a media magnet or the party establishment's pick. Anyone who is neither will be the longest of long shots.

The arduous nature of the nomination process hurts the administration of public business. The money needed and the process's length lead to political leaders neglecting their current duties for an extended period of time to run for president. In addition, public policy issues ought to be based on what is right for the American people. Instead, public policy issues are cast in the light of presidential elections. This posturing begins two years before the election.

The long campaign and its forced resolution guarantee the party is at war with itself from the Spring of the year before the election until late Spring to early Summer of the year of the election. So often the difference between candidates comes down to style and personality, and the internal strife is often of the nastiest sort. This does not lead to a strong political party.

The frontloaded primary system leads to much wasted time, money, and votes. Campaigns that drop out within the first few contests waste money to obtain ballot access in every state and they waste the time their volunteers spent on collecting all the signatures to get on every state's ballot.

As for wasted votes, the best example of this was in the 2016 Arizona Republican Primary. Marco Rubio withdrew on March 15th after finishing in Florida. However, he won 12% of the vote seven days later due to early voting. Some voters intentionally vote for a withdrawn favorite, but many others feel disenfranchised when they cast an early vote and the candidate withdraws.

Another issue is the concern about open primaries that let anyone cast a vote for the Republican nominee and semi-open primaries that let unaffiliated independents vote in the Republican Primary. In past elections, these primaries have invited mischief. The most notable case was in 2000 when a Democratic State Representative organized Democrats to cross over in the GOP primary for John McCain to tweak Bush-supporting Governor John Engler. McCain won the state by seven points, so it's debatable how much the shenanigans affected the final outcome.

In 2008, Independents made a key difference in New Hampshire. Exit polls showed that Mitt Romney defeated McCain 35-34% among Republicans. McCain won because he garnered 40% of the Independent vote to Romney's

27%. McCain's strong showing among Independents led to a feeling that non-Republicans had hijacked the party's nominating system. Many conservatives felt this way about the 2016 nomination but had less evidence to support it.

In 2016, exit polls in the early modified closed open primary states of New Hampshire and South Carolina showed Trump winning the same share of the Republican and Independent votes. However, with different finishers through the rest of the field. Later states' exit polls showed the Republicans were less enthusiastic than Independent with some exceptions, such as in Virginia where Independents turned out in force against Trump. However, no state exit poll showed Trump winning the state on the strength of Independent.

The Independent voter has an understandable desire to have influence over who runs in the general election. However, it's a dubious policy for a party to allow people not committed to its values cancel out the votes of its committed members. In the past, there have been organized shenanigans to influence the elections as well as malicious crossover voters who admit to how they voted to sabotage the other party. Because of that, the winner of an open primary is open to the risk of being tainted in the eyes of party members who didn't vote for them.

Many fixes have been proposed to the nominating system. Many voters favor a national primary election date where the popular vote determines the winner. This would solve the problem of momentum forcing people to choose candidates they don't like. A simple national primary in late April or early May could also shorten the interminable length of the campaign.

A national primary would solve some problems of the current system. Certainly, voters wouldn't have to make their vote based on what other states did. However, a national primary would create many other problems and it would exacerbate others. If America switched to a national primary, only those with massive campaign funds and massive platforms (i.e. celebrity status) could compete, even more so than our current system. Many candidates could make the ballots with the result that someone wins with a very small percentage of the vote. In the eleven-candidate Iowa Caucus field, Ted Cruz won the caucus with only 28% of the vote. Imagine a party nominee who 70% of the party didn't vote for and that many might disapprove of.

In theory, these problems could be solved. The top two candidates could meet in a runoff election. To maintain opportunity for candidates who aren't independently wealthy celebrities or part of the political elite, the RNC could let Iowa, New Hampshire, and two other states keep their early contests. Only those candidates who finished in the top three in two different contests would be eligible for the national primary, and the early states would only vote in the runoff. There would be no delegates and no "Big Mo" to push voters in later states. The early states would be akin to the regular season with the national primary being the playoff and the runoff being the finals.

Whatever solutions are proposed for a national primary, it would have challenges that would make it most difficult to achieve. First is the financial difficulty. Most states hold a presidential primary on special dates already, but many others don't have a separate presidential primary in the first place.

While some complain caucuses are cumbersome, the reason many states utilize them is it saves the states the cost and expense of a primary. In my home state of Idaho, we spent $1.9 million on our state's special presidential primary. That would have paid the salary of ten highway patrolmen or eleven teachers for four years. A runoff makes it even more expensive.

Second is the political difficulty. Many special interests are against a national primary. The small states don't want a national primary or a national popular vote election for the president. Others fear the dilution of their state's interests. Regardless, it's unlikely you'd persuade all fifty state legislatures to go along with this idea and fund it.

Congress could pass a law mandating a national primary, but that'd be constitutionally dubious if the major parties were not on board. The Supreme Court has held that political parties have a First Amendment right to decide their own nominating process.

The RNC could draft a less ambitious reform which would do away with the frontloaded system, similar to 1976's relaxed schedule than the numerous Super Tuesdays occurring in March of 2016. However, that would require a fundamental shift of philosophy. Until then, the GOP nominee will always either be the darling of the political establishment or the media.

New Party, Old System

How would a new party go about nominating its presidential candidates? Minor parties haven't utilized most states' primary systems. For the most part, they've used the convention system that arose with the 1832 election. Voters at the grassroots level choose delegates to attend the national convention to choose the presidential and vice-presidential nominees of the party at State Conventions, with the delegates from the State Conventions being elected at local or county party meetings.

Rather than having the nominee dictated by the media or political bosses, the party's nominee for the presidency is decided by delegates chosen by the grassroots of the party. This solves many problems of the existing primary system used by the major parties. It doesn't force states to make decisions based on what other states have done. It avoids spending hundreds of millions of dollars on attacking other party leaders.

The convention system does have room for twenty-first century improvements in the process, but it definitely works as a starting place.

A new political party could invent its own way of choosing its nominee, but that's fraught with peril. In 1996, the Reform Party did a national mail-in primary. The losing candidate's supporters alleged fraud had occurred, and this began the disintegration of the Reform Party. While there's no evidence fraud occurred, it's easy to understand how such a system may be open to fraud. A new political party is not making a wise decision when it decides to invent a new system of choosing presidential nominees while getting established.

Improvements would be appropriate as a new party grows. Such changes may include a system of presidential primaries or even a ranked choice voting system that serves as an instant runoff. Hopefully, when that time comes, the new party will plan its primaries to avoid the pitfalls the Republicans have built into their system.

One change that could be implemented far quicker than new primaries is to expand national conventions. In all parties, the national convention works the way it has since the 1830s, with delegates coming from across the country to a single convention site. While some will always find it desirable for people to meet, hold committee hearings, and be physically in the same place, in the twenty-first century, participation can and should be made simpler.

To attend the major party conventions as a delegate can cost three-to-five thousand dollars. This limits participation. Virtual delegates could be elected from communities across America and meet at central locations in their own states to cast floor votes for President and Vice-President, as well as the platform and other national party issues. This would allow more participation and ensure delegates were accountable to the grassroots for their decisions.

Regardless, a new political party will produce a better system than the Republicans and Democrats have. At least it would be hard to do worse.

Chapter 5
We'll Never Join You!

Some have suggested that, if conservatives dislike Donald Trump, then we should join the Democrats. With many of us, this provokes an *Empire Strikes Back* response: "We'll never join you!"

Let's be clear. It's foolish and counterproductive to refuse to join hands with political and ideological rivals when we do have issues and concerns in common. This is true whether it's free speech or the belief in basic democratic norms that President Trump often undermines.

Yet there's a difference between joining hands on an issue and belonging to the same party. In past generations, crossing over from one party to another was not impossible because there were basic values that members of both parties shared. That's no longer the case today.

The Democrats are increasingly hostile towards people of certain faiths. Joining the Democrats will offer you no challenges, if your faith allows you to bend towards whatever beliefs are advocated by modern liberalism and to only voice your faith in your house of worship or in support of leftwing polices on welfare, health care, and immigration.

If you hold to traditional Judeo-Christian moral standards and your faith influences you more than a political ideology, then you have a problem. (In fact, you will also have a problem in the modern GOP in different ways but we'll discuss that later.) During the Obama Administration, arguments of "live and let live" on issues like birth control, chemical abortions, and same-sex marriage became, "Do what we say or we will bankrupt you."

While some Republicans do cross the line into making bigoted statements against Blacks, Hispanics, and Muslims, the Democrats have their own strains of bigotry. While Republicans disowned the belief observant Catholics can't be trusted with high government positions, Democrats have embraced this belief with fervor.

A Democrat on the Senate Judiciary Committee, Diane Feinstein (D-CA) attacked the Catholic Judge Amy Comey-Barrett by saying, "The dogma lives loudly within you."

Senator Kamela Harris, a leading Democratic Presidential candidate, has challenged another Catholic judicial nominee because of his membership in the Catholic Charitable organization the Knights of Columbus.

In addition, a strain of anti-Semitism exists in many progressive circles. Many on the left refuse to disavow figures like Nation of Islam founder Louis Farrakhan who justified his anti-Jewish and anti-Israel stances by saying on Twitter, "I'm not anti-Semite, I'm anti-termite."

This anti-Semitism has been given new life by Rep. Ilhan Omar (D-MN) who suggested members of Congress are bought and paid for by a bi-partisan Israel lobby. This is an obvious dog whistle for the anti-Semitic idea that Jews are using money to control the world. She was forced to make a weak apology which claimed ignorance for her statement. However, this was not the case. She had a history of making these statements before the election. Not she is in her thirties and spent four years in a refugee camp in Somalia while she was growing up.

Democratic Minnesota State Senator Ron Latz gave Omar the benefit of the doubt and invited her to his home, where she met with leaders of the local Jewish Community for two hours.

"We shared with her our concerns for things, including language that has references and meanings beyond just the meanings of words. Tropes, dog whistles—call them what you will. We explained to her how hurtful, and factually inaccurate, they were."

Despite these efforts, Latz and others have noted she continues on an irresponsible course, and House Democrats let her get off with an apology that, at its core, was a lie. It's worth noting that just before Omar's statement on Twitter, Republicans punished Rep. Steve King (R-IA) by stripping him of all of his committee assignments after some racially charged comments.

Not every Democrat is an anti-Semite, just as not every Republican is a racist. However, Republicans remain willing to tolerate a degree of racism if it helps them win. Democrats likewise will tolerate anti-Semitism to win. There are minority Republicans and Jewish Democrats who offer explanations of why bigotry is wrong, but at the end of the day, the reality is the major parties point fingers at each other while both refuse to root out all bigotry, believing they can't win without their own party's "tolerable" bigoted wing.

Abortion is another key issue for conservatives and a growing number of Americans. Medical science's advances since 1973 have made Justice Harry Blackmunn's attempt to delineate the medical circumstances under which a pregnancy can be terminated seem like voodoo compared to the stark truths presented by modern ultrasound technology.

Despite the ever-increasing evidence of the unborn child's humanity, the Democratic Party's heart grows harder and harder on the issue. It was less than a generation ago that Bill Clinton proclaimed his goal that abortion be "safe, legal, and rare."

In recognizing the need for abortion to be "rare," Clinton acknowledged that abortion was tragic. This reassured moderate pro-choicers and pro-lifers who aren't single-issue voters that President Clinton understood that abortion wasn't a good thing.

Today's Democratic Party can hardly be seen as believing that. They're against any restriction on abortion up until the moment of birth. Regulations to protect women's health are viewed as unconstitutional impediments. Pro-Abortion Democratic women now proclaim they are glad they had abortions. Clinton's statement would be seen as too mild and milquetoast.

Pro-life Democrats exist but they tend to crumble under pressure from their party. A prime example is when President Obama compelled his party's pro-life wing to allow the passage of the abortion-promoting affordable care act. In recent decades, almost to a person, "pro-life" Democrats refuse to pull federal funds from America's largest abortion provider Planned Parenthood, won't stand up for the confirmation of judges who will overturn Roe v. Wade, and support politicians who represent the most radical pro-abortion positions. "Pro-Life" Democratic Senator Bob Casey has a 74% lifetime rating from the Planned Parenthood Action fund.

Yet, despite their total ineffectiveness at being pro-life, Democratic Party Chairman Tom Perez in April 2017 declared support for abortion rights "non-negotiable." If we support even the most basic restrictions on abortion, the Democratic Party is no home for us.

On economics, America's national debt is more than $20 trillion and is heading for fiscal disaster. If the Republicans are sending us over the cliff at 80 MPH, the Democrats want to hit the accelerator and take it up to 100 MPH. As of this writing, Senator Bernie Sanders (I-VT) has produced his Medicare for All bill in Congress with many Democratic co-sponsors including relative moderates like Cory Booker (D-NJ). The Center for a Responsible Federal Budget studied Sanders' similar plan from 2016 and estimated it would cost the country $2.6 and $13.7 trillion and raise the national debt to between 100 and 150 percent of GDP.

At the core of the Democratic Party's message is an abandonment of the idea we fix Social Security and Medicare despite nightmarish fiscal projections.

During the 1990s, Democrats like Bill Clinton and Senators John Breaux (D-LA) and Daniel Patrick Moynihan (D-NY) knew the system was headed for crisis but they were stymied by the left wing of their party and Clinton's own misbehavior in office. Today's Democrats chose the path of trying to scare seniors and keep the system as-is even though that will soon give us a lose-lose choice of either severely cutting benefits or raising SSI premiums to 80% of a worker's wages in order to keep supporting our existing retiree population.

On foreign policy, the Obama Administration provided no leadership. We saw the rise of ISIS because President Obama and the left underestimated them and called them "the J.V. Squad." President Obama led the most anti-Israel administration in U.S. history. Obama has publicly disrespected Israel's Prime Minister and in his waning days in office, Obama let a one-sided, anti-Israel UN Security Council resolution pass.

Obama spent most of his administration in a passive posture towards the cyberattacks and the aggressiveness of Russia and China. His administration lied to the American people about the true case of the Benghazi terror attacks. President Obama refused to name America's enemies in the world, instead trying to find new politically correct phrases for what the Bush Administration termed "the War on Terror."

If you support a responsible foreign policy, the Democratic Party is no home for you. The Democrats' weak foreign policy made America less safe during the Obama years and lowered America's standing with key allies such as the U.K. and Israel.

The one possible counter to the argument the Democrats are unsuited for governing is that Trump's recklessness represents a unique challenge to democratic norms. Despite their faults, the Democrats still claim to believe in norms that the Republicans no longer uphold. Grassroots Democrats across America sincerely mean it, but I've got reasons to doubt that goes for their political leaders and establishment as well as much of the activist class.

Liberals decry the President declaring critical news outlets such as the major networks and the New York Times to be "fake news." It's pointed out that free speech and the free press exists as a check on political power. Yet most of them didn't protest when President Obama attacked Fox News as fake news or when President Clinton went after Rush Limbaugh by name.

President Trump can't focus on doing his job while he opines on things that aren't his job and inflame division in this country unnecessarily. Yet, he's just extending the steps of President Obama who commented on the latest antics of Kanye West at one point in his presidency and started a needlessly controversy when he inserted himself into a dispute between a professor and a Connecticut police officer, judging that the officer had acted "stupidly."

Obama and his supporters often played the race card, against opposition to the President based upon his policies. A CNN/ORC poll in October 2016 found 54% of American felt racial relations had worsened between blacks and whites during the Obama Administration.

What of executive orders? Many on the left are concerned that Trump is abusing his power, yet had no problem when Obama governed by executive orders to evade an uncooperative Republican Congress. Obama unilaterally attempted to impose amnesty and changes in welfare reform rather than work through the legislative process laid out in the Constitution. He declared he had a pen and a phone and would use them to make changes Congress didn't want.

In an article in the Atlantic, McKay Poppins noted McMullin appeared at a recording of the liberal Slate podcast *Gabfest* before a live audience and made a case for limited government. Poppins quotes McMullin as saying, "We're in this moment here where we have a president who absolutely has authoritarian tendencies, and you're still arguing for a large, centralized government. Now is a moment where we may want to rethink that." Poppins then writes, "It was a good line, and McMullin's delivery begged for applause. What he got instead was a solitary whoo echoing across an otherwise silent theater."

This suggests many Democrats are less concerned about a dangerous all-powerful state that endangers personal liberty and more concerned that their side isn't running it.

As for ethics in government, the Democrats have a long list of issues from the House Post Office and House Bank scandals of the 1990s, to Charlie Rangel (D-NY). The Chairman of the Tax-writing House Ways and Means Committee spent decades violating the public trust in many ways—including evading taxes. Congressman Bill Jefferson (D-LA) was convicted of bribery after he had been found to have stowed more than $100,000 in bribe money in a freezer. New York Governor Elliot Spitzer ran an anti-corruption campaign for Governor only to be forced out when he got caught in a series of liaisons with high priced call girls a little more than a year after taking office.

A detailed history of all of the Democrats' ethics violations would be tedious and depressing. The top peak of Democratic corruption and the most relevant to the Trump corruption in the GOP are the Bill and Hillary Clinton. The Clintons' history of corruption is long, detailed, and complicated. Writing entire books about the corrupt dealings of the Clintons is a cottage industry on the right.

Some charges are dubious, even kooky. Just as people create tall tales of virtue about great leaders like Washington and Lincoln, people create tall tales of vice about Trump and the Clintons. I'm going to avoid rehashing the 1990s in their entirety and focus on the actions of Mrs. Clinton, since she is the spouse still active in seeking political office.

Hillary Clinton may be her husband's chief enabler. When allegations began to surface that her husband had an affair with an intern young enough to be his daughter, President Clinton lied under oath about it in a civil trial and he encouraged others to lie as well. She dismissed the allegations as the result of a "vast right-wing conspiracy," a signal to the Democrats to rally around the President regardless of the facts.

Her own political future was tied to his. Her defense was an unspoken argument. *If his wife doesn't care, why should we?* She was his enabler. Yet, from multiple allegations, she was not just enabling his consensual affairs, but his abuse of other women. Donald Trump reminded the public of this when he had a press conference before a debate that featured three women who had accused President Clinton of sexual assault, harassment, and rape.

Being an enabler has paid off. New York's senior senator Daniel Patrick Moynihan retired in 2000, and Mrs. Clinton ran for his seat. Mrs. Clinton was not a New Yorker and had never lived in the state. The Illinois-born former first lady of Arkansas, using the obvious dishonesty which was the hallmark of her public career, declared, "I've always been a Yankees fan."

As implausible as that was, the New York Democratic Party establishment cleared the field to make her New York's junior senator.

Representing New York was a big boon to Senator Clinton's presidential ambitions as it gave her easy access to big donors, including Donald Trump, and her tenure was building towards a 2008 Presidential run. Almost the entire Democratic Party establishment rallied to her side. A funny thing happened on the way to her coronation. Grassroots Democrats turned against Clinton. One ad by Obama fans compared her to the George Orwell's Big Brother.

She became known for her outlandish lies in 2008, after she invented an incident where she landed under sniper fire in Bosnia and had to run under fire to a vehicle to reach a base.

In addition, her 2008 campaign sank to attempting to use Obama's race against him. In a 2015 column, liberal columnist Ryan Cooper said she needed to address the racist overtones of her previous campaign. She didn't, as her preference seems to be to paper over problematic elements of her history.

She was appointed as Secretary of State by Obama where she famously offered a reset button to the Russian foreign minister. Late in her tenure, the American embassy in Benghazi, Libya came under attack. Secretary Clinton furthered a false narrative that the attack was the result of a YouTube video that had angered Muslims, even telling this lie to the victims' families.

Corruption colored her tenure at the State Department in many ways. One way was the non-profit foundation she and President Clinton set up after they left the Whitehouse. The Clinton Foundation has admitted to violations of the ethics rules by accepting money from the Algerian government while Secretary Clinton was America's top diplomat. Throughout her campaign, the Clinton Foundation looked increasingly like a way for the rich and powerful to gain influence with her without the pesky limits and requirements of campaign finance law.

To ensure public accountability and national security, State Department Employees are required to use a government email server. To avoid public accountability and to ensure she controlled what emails became public, Hillary Clinton used her private email server run out of a bathroom closet in Denver.

Found on the server were eighty-one instances of classified information, and 2,000 more documents have now been retroactively classified. Clinton put America's national security at risk so she could restrict what emails would be available for public review. Mishandling classified information as she did has led to jail time for less well-connected citizens than Secretary Clinton.

Secretary Clinton's public approval rating sank and she found herself once again losing state after state. This time, it wasn't a young rock star Senator from Illinois who challenged her but 74-year-old Bernie Sanders. He had run campaigns for Governor in Senate in the 1970s as a left-wing crank before being elected Mayor of Burlington, Vermont and winning election to the House in the 1990s and to the Senate in 2006. Sanders, a self-declared socialist, was the fringiest of fringe candidates—and he nearly beat Hillary Clinton. He continued to beat her or to lose at a narrow margin late into the process. Clinton had to fight Sanders almost to the Convention.

Just before the convention, Wikileaks revealed the Democratic National Committee had been on Clinton's side, running interference for her campaign in the media and helping her formulate campaign strategy. This forced Democratic National Committee Chairwoman Debbie Wasserman-Schultz to resign on the eve of the Democratic National Convention. She was replaced by former Al Gore strategist Donna Brazile. It came out later that Brazile also helped the Clinton campaign. During the primary, she was working as a contributor to CNN. She forwarded along information the Sanders campaign had sent the media, giving Clinton a "heads up." More importantly, she leaked Town Hall topics to Secretary Clinton in advance of joint appearances with Sanders.

Note one key difference between the two major parties. Both nominated people of bad personal character. The Republicans nominated Trump because of a lack of cohesion, vision, and lack of any reliable sense of leadership within the Party establishment. The Democrats nominated Hillary Clinton with the full-throated support of the political establishment, including the unethical interference and influence of the DNC.

Secretary Clinton almost got away with it, too. She was, after all, running against Donald Trump. One flaw shipwrecked her campaign: arrogance. The Clintons had always thrived by living in the legal and ethical gray area. While their associates often went to prison, they walked away scot free or with punishments that didn't seem to hurt them. President Clinton was disbarred for his perjury and subordination of perjury in the *Jones v. Clinton* lawsuit but he never intended to practice law again and the media didn't cover it as huge, so few people cared. The Clintons are not like other people.

That bring us to September 9, 2016, the night, at an LGBT gala, Clinton identified half of Trump's supporters as "a basket of deplorables." Some truly awful people did support Trump, such as Richard Spencer and the rest of the alt-right, but they numerically aren't half of Trump supporters. Clinton had identified who she viewed as deplorable as "The racist, sexist, homophobic, xenophobic, Islamophobic."

By 2016, those terms had been hurled at any opponent of liberal ideology or practical government until they were practically meaningless. A racist was someone who didn't like Obamacare. A sexist is anyone who didn't like Hillary Clinton. A homophobe is anyone who held the same views in opposition to same sex marriage that both Hillary Clinton and Barack Obama held prior to 2012. A xenophobe protested the sanctuary cities protecting the people who commit felonies like rape and murder while living in the USA illegally. An Islamophobe was anyone bothered by Obama's feckless response to radical Islamist extremists and ISIS.

The Trump campaign played the "deplorables" sound bite perfectly. For many Americans on the fence and concerned by Trump, the "deplorables" comment confirmed Hillary Clinton and her supporters held them and many Americans like them in contempt. It crystallized Hillary Clinton's greatest flaw: more than dishonesty, more than the casual corruption, what brought Clinton down was her ceaseless arrogance.

That arrogance led her to the loss of three states that had been voting for Democratic Presidential candidates for decades. Hilary Clinton was the first Democrat to lose Pennsylvania and Michigan since Michael Dukakis in 1988, and the first Democrat to lose Wisconsin since Walter Mondale lost 49 states in 1984. She didn't bother to visit Wisconsin during the campaign but did manage to hold multiple big events in New York City on Broadway.

At the end of the day, America faced a bad choice between two terrible candidates. Republicans forfeited their credibility on the issue of character and integrity in public office in 2016, but the Democrats did the same thing two decades before and have shown no sign of sincere remorse. There's no reason to join either one of them, and every reason to demand better options.

Truth be told, honest liberals and center leftist deserve their own political party free of the corruption of the Democrats. I hope someone on the left seriously undertakes that effort.

Chapter 6
Imagine There Were No Parties...

It's a line John Lennon never wrote in his classic "Imagine" but many wish he did. In America, our political parties have become warring rival tribes. Both the Republicans and the Democrats have become home to ambitious, self-serving people and political radicals out of touch with basic reality.

If you are apprehensive about political parties, you're in good company. Many of America's Founding Fathers were not fans. In his farewell address, George Washington himself warned of the dangers of regional based political parties, saying:

> However combinations or associations of the above description may now and then answer popular ends, they are likely, in the course of time and things, to become potent engines, by which cunning, ambitious, and unprincipled men will be enabled to subvert the power of the people and to usurp for themselves the reins of government, destroying afterwards the very engines which have lifted them to unjust dominion.

Later in his address, Washington warned of the dangers of "the spirit of party" in general:

> The alternate domination of one faction over another, sharpened by the spirit of revenge, natural to party dissension, which in different ages and countries has perpetrated the most horrid enormities, is itself a frightful despotism. But this leads at length to a more formal and permanent

despotism. The disorders and miseries which result gradually incline the minds of men to seek security and repose in the absolute power of an individual; and sooner or later the chief of some prevailing faction, more able or more fortunate than his competitors, turns this disposition to the purposes of his own elevation, on the ruins of public liberty.

America's second President John Adams wrote in a letter in 1780:

> There is nothing which I dread so much as a division of the republic into two great parties, each arranged under its leader, and concerting measures in opposition to each other. This, in my humble apprehension, is to be dreaded as the greatest political evil under our Constitution.

Many of the Founders were critical of the danger of political parties but nevertheless became members of America's first political parties. The Democratic Republicans counted among their membership Thomas Jefferson and James Madison, the author of the Declaration of Independence and the Father of the Constitution. The Federalist Party had Madison's *Federalist Papers* Co-Author Alexander Hamilton and the previously quoted John Adams.

Despite the dangers of political parties, most of the Founders ended up concluding they were a necessary evil. The chief reason political parties exist is people have different ideas as to how the government should operate. Thomas Jefferson came to see political parties as more or less natural and healthy as he wrote in a 1798 letter:

> in every free & deliberating society, there must from the nature of man be opposite parties, & violent dissensions & discords; and one of these for the most part must prevail over the other for a longer or shorter time. perhaps this party division is necessary to induce each to watch & debate to the people the proceedings of the other.

Parties are formed because people have strong disagreements. However, political parties don't have to be destructive. If they are functional, they serve to promote the interests of liberty by acting as a check on one another. The problem is America's two parties are not functional, so they are serving to eat away at our liberties.

An effective political party would organize activists, voters, and resources efficiently in opposition to both the Republicans and the Democrats. A good political party begins to form a memory of who its supporters and activists are. Running Independent Candidates is often more expensive and less effective.

Imagine Candidate A runs as an Independent for State Senate in the 2018 elections and loses. Candidate B runs in 2020 with the same platform and a similar temperament. Candidate B's campaign has to build their organization from scratch and form their own campaign team. They'll have none of the data on Candidate A's campaign in terms of which voters had been friendly. They'll spend a lot of time reinventing the wheel and doing work that would have been unnecessary had both A and B belonged to the same political party.

Competent political parties keep track of people they identify as friendly to their cause. They provide a ready source of activists who are active in the party and have worked on previous campaigns. A party can build its operations more easily from one election to another.

It's easier to run as a candidate of a party rather than as an Independent. For example, in my home state of Idaho, if you're a member of either of the two major parties or our two recognized minor parties, you can file for office simply by paying a filing fee. For example, it's $300 to file to run for Congress or $30 to run for the state legislature. An Independent candidate must collect signatures in order to get on the ballot.

A little-known candidate of a minor party has seven months to make their case to voters and increase their name recognition if they're the only candidate the party is running, which is common. If you're an independent, you have to beat the streets to get enough signatures in the middle of March to even have a chance of appearing on the ballot in November.

An independent candidacy is appropriate as a one-time challenge to the two major parties. If citizens wish to mount a long-term challenge, they can best do so with a party of their own and this should be their long-term goal.

While a new party may be necessary, it's not necessary to emulate the excessive "spirit of party" that exists in both the major parties.

Passions have always run strong in our political system. In some ways, this is necessary and even good for a Republic. Yet, the debate has turned ugly. We've not merely debated ideas, we've debased people.

It was seen in people comparing President Bush to Hitler. It was seen in a post on the left-wing *Democratic Underground* where a poster wrote of pulling over to the side of the road to help a stranded motorist only to speed away over the Bush bumper sticker on the motorist's car. The Internet is filled with trashy, tasteless pictures and posts mocking first lady Michelle Obama for her appearance. And now the ugliness can be seen in the right embracing Donald Trump in hopes he truly will make America great again.

There's little evidence they understand what debases America or where American greatness came from. It came from American goodness. American greatness was the brave few struggling to keep the flame of liberty alive at a cold Valley Forge without any shoes. It was a twenty-year-old Nathan Hale declaring, "I only regret that I have but one life to lose for my country."

American greatness was George Washington spurning a crown so that the Republic could live. It was Abraham Lincoln on the eve of victory in the Civil War calling for it to end "with malice towards none and charity for all."

American greatness was our nation coming together as one to fight the evils of Nazi Germany and Imperial Japan. Great Americans fought bravely at Midway, Normandy, and Iwo Jima. At the end of the War, America could have taken spoils but instead we fed and nourished the peoples who had been at war with us and nursed their broken nations back to the health. That was the greatness of America.

American greatness brought the change wrought by the peaceful, non-violent Civil Rights movement. It was President Reagan standing against the Russian "Evil Empire" and bringing it to its knees without firing a shot.

America doesn't always live up to its best. When it does, when we see America display courage and goodness, it reminds us of why so many of our ancestors risked everything to come here. It reminds us to be loyal to that vision of America at its best above all else.

A new political party should honor that vison by showing respect for our nation's highest principles and all its citizens, including those who disagree with them. I'm not naïve enough to suggest a political party not challenge its opponents on the issues or never declare that a policy is so wrongheaded, it's dangerous. A political party should call out unethical conduct by politicians of other parties and not tolerate corruption from its own.

However, abusive, violent rhetoric and petty personal attacks dominate today's political scene. These are not necessary nor helpful, nor is mindless opposition and obstruction. Consider Senate Democrats who drug their feet on allowing President Trump's cabinet nominees a floor vote in 2017. Many of these nominees were confirmed with a supermajority support which laid bare the fact the Democrats only blocked them for partisan purposes.

Not every act by another party merits our criticism, anger, attack, or opposition. Sometimes, a politician from another party has a good idea and being magnanimous is a better approach.

Finally, it's important for anew party to push back against the ways both major parties have sought to strip away neutral ground. Everything is political. Much of this is thanks to left-wing activists who have politicized even sports, thus undermining a happy distraction for the American people in troubled times. Other left-wing activist groups have pushed politicizing the holidays by preparing talking points for young liberals to lobby their older relatives to support Obamacare on Thanksgiving.

Left-wing activists have sunk to harassing politicians and their families in restaurants. Right-wing anti-Communists formed a threatening mob that went after Nancy Pelosi and shouted curses at her. A new party needs to reject the destructive mobs on the left and the right.

Americans need common ground. We need peaceful moments free from partisan battles. We can't expect a rational and civil political conversation when every public space is a battleground. People need to be able to get away from the political mess. A new party should stand for spaces free of political attacks and full of non-partisan good will. A new party should actively foster that and stand in opposition to efforts to politicize every moment.

While some might agree it's best for political activists to be part of a party, you may ask, why start a new party? After all, there are at least two existing national third parties the discontented can join. We'll examine those parties in our next chapter.

Chapter 7
No Time for Losing

Once we've concluded neither of the two major parties is acceptable, the question becomes, why not join one of the existing minor parties? That would avoid having to start from scratch on party-building, particularly ballot access, which will remain a key challenge for any third party. Each of the states has a system built with access for the two major parties in mind, and has a varying degree of tolerance for minor party and Independent candidates.

The Constitution Party, founded in 1991, has ballot access in the critical swing state of Florida, along with over twenty other states. The Libertarians have been around since 1976 and are skilled at getting their party's nominees on the ballot. Their 2016 nominee Gary Johnson was the only third-party candidate on the ballot in all 50 states.

Further, the Libertarian and Constitution party platforms do reflect some Conservative values. Yet the Libertarian Party is known for social tolerance bordering on licentiousness. The party favors legal availability of prostitution, pot, and pornography. If that alone doesn't give you pause, consider the 2016 Libertarian Party Convention where, while the delegates were in the process of casting votes for Vice-President, they were treated to a strip tease most neither wanted nor expected.

James Weeks was an obese candidate for National Chairman of the Libertarian Party when he came on the stage and did a strip tease down to his underwear in front of the entire convention and a national television audience.

The 2016 election was a grand opportunity for the Libertarian Party to establish itself as a serious political force. Weeks' behavior illustrates why this didn't happen. It would not be fair to suggest Weeks' actions represents all Libertarians. After the convention, the Libertarian Party of Michigan expelled Weeks. Yet, it's fair to ask how Weeks got there.

Weeks was not only a candidate for national party chairman, he had been the 2014 Libertarian nominee for the U.S. House. In 2016, he was his party's candidate for County Sheriff. Understanding how Weeks got on that stage is critical, particularly if you're thinking about joining either of the two existing minor parties that appeal to people on the political right.

While joining existing third parties is worth considering, this superficially easier move is not a wise strategy if you're wanting to effect change. Before we look at more evidence of this, let me be clear. Many sincere Libertarian Party members are deeply concerned about the issues. Every four years, hundreds of thousands of Americans vote for the Libertarian Party Presidential nominee. They represent the values of a significant number of Americans.

Given that, it's surprising how few Libertarian candidates run for office. In 2016, the Libertarians ran over 600 candidates for federal, state, and local offices. That's not impressive when one considers the countless thousands of positions that were up: school boards, city councils, county commissions, state legislatures, Congress, and more.

As such, it's too easy for embarrassing extremists to rise unimpeded to become a candidate for the chief law enforcement officer of a county or a candidate for National Party leadership. In most of the country where the Libertarian or Constitution Parties are on the ballot, if you have a pulse and can pay the filing fee, you can be the party's nominee for any local office you wish. Most of the time, you can run for the U.S. House without opposition in the Libertarian primary.

Libertarian and Constitution Party candidates outside of the Presidential race are not at all representative of the best candidates possible from within the party. Rather, they are a coalition of warm bodies willing to fill a role.

A successful political party is made of many different types of people:

- Peacekeepers form a coalition of folks with divergent views, make everyone feel respected, and unite the party on common ground.

- Confident candidates value voters' opinions and care about their lives.

- Visionaries rally the party and inspire while reflecting party values.

- Persuaders help raise funds and build the party infrastructure.

- Organizers strategize plans for the phone banks, the ground game, and Internet outreach.

- Principled idealists hold the party leadership to account and keep the party from abandoning its values for a mere quest for political power.

The last group annoys major parties' leadership but they serve a needed role. However, the Libertarian and Constitution Parties suffer from having too many idealists. In large numbers, idealists tend to become militant and clash with each other. In addition, the need for warm bodies can force them into positions they're ill-suited for. A "take no prisoners" political brawler doesn't belong in a position that requires bringing people together. Yet such people end up the party nominees since they are more likely to sacrifice the time and energy required to run.

To run a campaign for local office and to do it properly takes a massive commitment of time and energy. A Libertarian candidate for Governor or Senate knows, if they quit their job, spend nine months on the road not seeing their family, and beg constantly for money, they may get up to six percent of the vote. If they're charismatic, or if they have a few extra million dollars to drop, that may increase their gains to ten to twelve percent of the vote.

Consequentially, Libertarian and Constitution Party candidates often run poor campaigns. They expect to lose and thus speak with no filters, no effort to articulate their ideas in a way that won't offend the voters they need on their side to win.

It's a popular among third parties to believe their presidential candidates do poorly because they aren't allowed to debate. While the Commission on Presidential Debates is corrupt, if being in the debates would help third party candidates win, then why hasn't it helped? In races for Congress, Governor, and Senate, local news organizations have opened the doors to active third-party candidates without the stringent and unfair restrictions of the CPD. In some cases, after entering a debate, third-party candidates have gone down in the polls.

Third parties have been unable to establish legitimate political leaders in their own ranks, so increasingly they've turned to people who have won under major party banners. The Constitution Party nominated former Rep. Virgil Goode in 2012. The Green Party chose former Rep. Cynthia McKinney as its nominee in 2008. The Libertarians chose former Rep. Ron Paul in 1988, former Rep. Bob Barr in 2008, and former Governor Gary Johnson in 2012 and in 2016.

Except for Johnson, all these nominees had lost their last primary within their own party and been driven out. All were political has-beens at the time of their third-party nominations, although Paul got a second political life when he was re-elected to the House in 1996—as a Republican.

In Johnson's last Republican primary, he quit before he could lose in spectacular fashion. After ten years out of office, he had decided to run for President in the Republican Primary and excited no real interest. He was mired in single digits when he left the GOP to run as a Libertarian. He won the Libertarian nomination and finished with 1% of the vote.

Now, a new party should be open to nominating former office holders elected under other party's banners. If a former Congressman or Governor wishes to make a political comeback and they're a good candidate who holds the party's values, then do nominate them for an appropriate office. That said, the Presidential nominee is the whole party's standard bearer. That position shouldn't be given to someone whose only qualification is they held office once and their old party doesn't want anything to do with them.

However, 2016 offered the Libertarians a grand chance, with many Republican and Democratic voters disgruntled with their nominees. Libertarians could have chosen Austin Peterson, a thirty-something activist well-suited to a frustrated electorate. Instead they re-nominated Johnson and added to the ticket the long-time politician William Weld, whose record on the issues as Governor of Massachusetts included gun-control and was far from libertarian.

The Johnson-Weld ticket is what happens when people who don't know how to win make a pragmatic choice. They made executive experience a big deal in an election where no one cared. Many were looking for a protest vote. What's more, the Johnson-Weld ticket's experience was a bit stale. Johnson had been out of office since January 2003, and Weld hadn't been a governor since Windows '95 was the latest revolutionary technology.

The ticket's boosters showed tasteless cluelessness and lacked seriousness in promoting the duo with the motto, "Feel the Johnson," a slang term for a feeling a man's genitals. The official campaign wasn't much better.

A traditional libertarian such as Petersen would have appealed to both sides. In general, Peterson was socially liberal but without the tendency to force his views on others. He respected the rights of those who disagree with things like same-sex marriage. In addition, Peterson could have done better among disaffected Republicans because he was pro-life.

Not so for the Johnson/Weld ticket. Johnson opposed efforts to stop the government from forcing wedding photographers and cake makers to participate in same sex weddings, saying, "I mean under the guise of religious freedom, anybody can do anything." The message from Gary Johnson? "You can't trust those religious people with freedom of conscience."

Utah was a state that Donald Trump remained unpopular in throughout the election and Utah was the most likely to vote against him in high numbers. Johnson offended members of the Church of Jesus Christ of Latter-Day saints with the statement, "Back to Mormonism. Why shouldn't somebody be able to shoot somebody else because their freedom of religion says that God has spoken to them and that they can shoot somebody dead."

Johnson later claimed he'd meant to reference the days when Mormons were killed for their faith by other religious groups with government approval, but the damage was done. His double-digit polling numbers in Utah slipped away after Evan McMullin announced his Independent candidacy.

In some ways, Johnson's opinion on religious liberty mattered little. He might not like laws that protect religious liberty but if he appointed justices who strictly interpret the Constitution, they would uphold the laws on religious liberty. He pledged to do this in a town hall with Weld. However, when Weld was asked what type of people they had in mind, he named liberal Supreme Court Justices like Stephen Breyer and Merrick Garland. If conservatives wanted Supreme Court Justices like that, they could just vote for Clinton.

Indeed, Johnson and Weld heaped praise on Obama, and Hillary Clinton to an extent, which made it even harder for them to win over conservatives. And many conservatives who had backed Johnson stepped away from him.

McMullin announced his candidacy in August and was embraced by Conservatives who'd been curious about Johnson. McMullin won nearly a million votes despite his late entry into the race. In an interview on Peterson's radio program, McMullin said he would not have run had the Libertarian Party nominated a real libertarian.

Johnson's only supporters were Libertarian Party diehards, disgruntled Bernie Sanders supporters, and a few Independent voters. Even some of these became bothered by Johnson's behavior as the campaign wore on. Johnson is a long-time Marijuana user who stopped violating federal law while running to be America's chief law enforcement officer. Yet, he often spaced out. A key turning point came in September when a reporter asked what he'd do about Aleppo, the Syrian city central to the Syrian Civil War. Johnson replied, "What is Aleppo?"

During another interview with a reporter in September, Johnson stuck his tongue out. The public took notice of Johnson's behavior. At the height of his popularity, Johnson was at more than 9% in polling averages. The behavior conservatives found off-putting assured he wouldn't get the 15% in poll averages required to make the Presidential debates.

If he had succeeded in giving people someone that they could vote for without being embarrassed, he would have easily cleared the 5% threshold for the Libertarians to receive Federal matching funds in 2020. Instead, Johnson received 3.27% of the vote, around one third of his polling high.

While this was the highest percentage of the vote received by a third party in twenty years, Johnson's showing remained a wasted opportunity. The Libertarian Party had existed for forty years. This was the best they could do against the most unpopular major party nominees in American history.

The Constitution Party campaign was no more problematic than usual. Their nominee, Darryl Castle, was probably the best candidate they could have run. The Constitution Party peaked in its Presidential candidates' popular vote total when Howard Philips won 0.19% of the vote in the 1996 Presidential election, back when they were the U.S. Taxpayers Party.

The CP achieved its highest level of ballot access in 2000 when Philips appeared on the ballot in 41 states. This had fallen to 25 states by 2016.

The party has been racked by internal schisms and is on a trajectory to follow the course of the Prohibition Party. Note the Prohibition Party peaked in 1892 when its national nominee won 2% of the vote and has slowly faded into irrelevance.

While not dead, the Prohibition Party only reported a presence in sixteen states in 2018 and it appeared on just three states ballots in 2016. In 2004, the party split and had two separate conventions, one of which was in someone's living room. Their 2016 convention was only a conference call. They've had exactly one candidate elected in this century, as a tax assessor.

Neither the Libertarian nor Constitution Parties produce much talent capable of playing a constructive role in the political process. The exceptions get drawn to the major parties. One man in my state of Idaho proved to be an effective organizer for the Libertarian Party, successfully recruiting candidates across the state. He ended up joining the GOP, not because he agreed with them more but because he had a better chance of doing any good in the GOP.

Similarly, after a defeat as the Constitution Party candidate for President in 2008, Chuck Baldwin joined the GOP and ran for Lieutenant Governor of Montana. Ron Paul returned to the GOP and won a seat in Congress. Austin Petersen left the Libertarian Party to run for U.S Senate in Missouri. Others such as Rep. Justin Amash (R-MI) align with the Libertarian Party ideologically but always run as Republicans because they like to actually get elected to office.

So the Libertarian and Constitution Parties produce losing candidates and serve as a home for has-been politicians. The Libertarian and Constitution Parties further can't retain the talent who do have the capability of making an impact on the political process.

Losing with Purpose

The perpetual losing of the Libertarian and Constitution Parties scares away those serious about winning, but some losing is necessary to build a new political party.

As ballot access is being established, activists and candidates are gaining experience, and the party is being built, a normal process for a party is to begin by losing elections. However, this needs to transition to winning more and more as time goes on.

A new party will require people at all levels who are willing to become political martyrs in hopes of building something greater down the road. This would be like the pilgrims willing that their efforts would serve as "stepping stones" to others for a great work.

This must not be mistaken for the losing done by the Libertarian and the Constitution Parties. Losing in these parties is Sisyphean. The mythical King

Sisyphus was punished in the underworld by forever having to roll a boulder uphill only for it to come rolling back down. He had to keep going back down and pushing the boulder up for all eternity.

Both of the best-known, long-time third parties have built up a political culture of perpetual losing. In the coming chapters, we'll examine the failures of these parties, as well as the major parties to discover how we can build a political party that will advocate for ideas that will improve our country and learn how to win elections in order to implement them.

Chapter 8
Should We Wait for the Major Parties
to Make It Easier to Defeat Them?

One argument against forming a new party is a new party is impractical until fundamental structural changes are made. We have a system where the candidate with the most votes on the first round of balloting wins. Until this is changed, third party candidates will be deemed spoilers and wasted votes. The solutions proffered to this include ranked-choice voting (which I support) and having multi-member Congressional Districts (which is worth exploring.)

However, the practical flaw is this requires bodies controlled by the two major parties to pass legislation to make it easier for minor parties to compete. We wouldn't need new parties if we had two major parties willing to consider proposals that would make the U.S. election system fairer. Making it easier for new parties to compete would also make it harder for themselves.

However, while our voting system is a challenge for a new party and its candidates, it's not insurmountable. Examples from history show us this.

In this chapter, I'll examine relatively successful Independent and third-party efforts. My listing a party or candidate as successful in no way implies I'm endorsing that candidate's platform or stating a candidate's election was necessarily good. I'm only stating the candidate or party was able to achieve victory under our current voting system and therefore it disproves the futility argument against a new political party.

Back in the 1890s, the Populist Party was a successful third party. They're best-remembered for the 1892 Presidential Campaign of former Congressman James B. Weaver, who only won five states. However, the Populist Party won multiple elections. At their peak, the Populists held twenty-two U.S. House Seats and five seats in the U.S. Senate. Keep in mind this was before Senators were popularly elected. To get Senators elected, the Populists had to win seats in the state legislatures. So the Populist Party was successful under our current voting system.

Granted, these elections occurred more than 100 years ago. However, the point is the Populist Party won all of these elections under the current system. If our first past the post voting system made third-party efforts pointless, then the Populist Party's victories should not have been possible.

Other factors may make victory more difficult for a new party than it was for the Populists in the 1890s, such as the explosive growth of mass media, the subsequent increase in campaign expenses, and the social engineering efforts to make third-party votes seem pointless. However, none of these problems will be solved by a change in the voting system.

In addition, there have been more recent triumphs where the two-party system hasn't gotten its way. Most of these show the two major parties can be beaten, but are of limited usefulness:

1954: The former Governor J. Strom Thurmond defeated an Incumbent Democratic Senator running as a write-in candidate.

1970: Senator Harry F. Byrd, Jr. (Va.) left the Democratic Party and was elected as an Independent.

1990: Third Party candidates Walter Hickel (AK) and Lowell Weiker (CT) were elected Governors in the same year that Bernie Sanders (I-VT) won his first term in the U.S. House.

2006: After losing his primary race, Sen. Joseph Lieberman (CT) ran as an Independent and defeated the Democratic and Republican nominees.

2010: After losing a primary to a Tea Party insurgent candidate, Senator Lisa Murkowski (R-AK) was re-elected as a write-in.

2010: Former U.S. Senator Lincoln Chaffee was elected Governor of Rhode Island as an Independent.

In each case, the Republican and Democratic Parties were thwarted, but the candidates who did the thwarting already had successful careers inside the two parties. Thurmond was a popular former Governor and segregationist presidential candidate in 1948. Byrd was an incumbent Democratic Senator whose father (Harry F. Byrd, Sr.) had been a five-term U.S. Senator. Hickell had been elected to a previous term as Governor as a Republican before being appointed to Richard Nixon's Cabinet. Weicker had been a three-term U.S. Senator. Lieberman was a three-term Senator who had run for Vice-President. Murkowski was a first-term incumbent and the daughter of a former Senator and Governor of Alaska. Chaffee was a former U.S. Senator and the son of a U.S. Senator and Governor.

Many of these elected officials' breaks with their parties were short-lived. Thurmond and Murkowski rejoined their major parties after the election. Byrd and Lieberman continued to caucus with the Democrats. Chaffee joined the Democratic Party in 2013 to lay the groundwork for a futile Presidential run. Hickel rejoined the GOP in 1994.

Sanders is an unusual case. He migrated to Vermont with many other New Yorkers as part of a trend that moved Vermont from a bastion of Yankee Republicanism to a left-wing state that elected an avowed Socialist like Sanders to Congress. His road to Congress began with quixotic bids for high public office in 1971, including runs for Governor and U.S. Senate. He was elected

Mayor of Burlington, Vermont in 1981 and lost a bid for Governor in 1986 and a bid for the U.S. House in 1988 before winning in 1990. Sanders' success was a case of persistence in a state that was rapidly evolving to the point that he would be considered a mainstream candidate. As most areas of the country are not evolving towards conservatives, his case is not that instructive.

Three cases offer good examples of how people outside the major parties can triumph:

1970: James Buckley (C-NY) defeated the incumbent Republican Senator Charles Goodell.

1994: Angus King (I-ME) was elected Governor of Maine and then re-elected in 1998, elected to the Senate in 2012 and re-elected in 2018.

1998: Jesse Venture (Ref-MN) was elected Governor of Minnesota.

These three cases are good examples. 1970 is a case of the Conservative Party taking advantage of a Liberal split between the Democratic Candidate and Senator Goodell, who was so far to the left that he won the nomination of the Liberal Party.

Minnesota's 1998 Gubernatorial election saw a pro-wrestler and former Mayor of Brooklyn Park, Minnesota, Ventura, defeat two strong candidates for the Republicans and Democrats. Ventura rose from the low double digits in early September to win a three-point victory over future U.S. Senator Norm Coleman (R-MN.)

The best example was the 1994 election of Angus King. He won the Governorship of Maine as an Independent in a tight, three-way race. He was re-elected with 59% of the vote and then proceeded to win a majority in his 2012 and 2018 U.S. Senate runs. In the Senate, King caucuses with Democrats so he can be on committees. Otherwise, he still functions as an Independent, having endorsed some of his Republican colleagues for re-election.

Aside from King's left-of-center politics, he is a good example of the type of candidate a new party should run: someone who can not only win, but competently govern and gain trust and support for the long-term.

There are reasons that each of these candidates won and overcame the system's bias in favor of the two major parties. However, the important thing for the purpose of our discussion is that they did overcome it.

The historical record proves our voting system presents a challenge to new political parties, but that challenge is not insurmountable. Those who are concerned about the direction America's two political parties are taking this country in need not wait for the parties driving us off a cliff to make it easier to challenge them. Rather, let's prepare to do the hard work to win under the current system until we are in a position to change it.

Chapter 9
If You Build It...

I love good movies, and I have a special place in my heart for that rare good movie about politics. Yet movies can give us a funny idea about how political reform can happen.

Take Frank Capra's classic film *Mr. Smith Goes to Washington*, one of my all-time favorites. In the film, a decent, patriotic American gets appointed to the Senate by his home state's corrupt governor because he's scorned as a simple-minded yokel who surely won't get his bearings during his few months as an interim Senator before a special election. The hero, Jefferson Smith, not only gets his bearings in Washington, he leads a movement from the Senate to break the power of his state's political machine.

It's a great movie for its patriotism and defense of American values from corruption, and the importance of people standing and fighting for what they believe is right. However, like many Hollywood movies about politics, it has a flawed idea of how a reform movement starts. That is, a leader emerges with power, platform, and influence, and the people rally to their side.

In real life, people with ability, intelligence, and money aren't looking for lost causes to throw themselves into. Senator Ben Sasse (R-NE) was a critic of Donald Trump and thought there needed to be a third-party challenge to him if he got the nomination. When Trump clinched it in May 2016, some became upset that Sasse wasn't willing to make that challenge himself.

His decision was understandable. He was a young Senator (44) with three young children. He also had just started his tenure in the Senate. A six-month Presidential bid would require an absence from his job and time away from his family with no party organization to help get out the vote and no fundraising apparatus. This was not attractive or likely to succeed.

There are principled, politically skilled people who could run campaigns for state and national offices, but good people don't have the bandwidth for pointless efforts.

If third party organizers want to take a cue from Hollywood, I'd suggest the movie *Field of Dreams* as a picture of a functional third-party effort. In that movie, Ray Kinsella hears a voice and builds a baseball field on his failing farm. He spends a lot of time clearing the field and waiting until, eventually, old-time baseball players emerge from the corn to play.

While the political results won't be so dramatic, the key to getting the best people to run is to build a party that provides the infrastructure and the support that makes winning an election possible. If you ask a quality person to run for office and prove you offer quality organizational support, you're more likely to get a yes than if all you can offer them is ballot access. We saw in the prior chapter what type of candidates you get that way.

What this means is people need to do their bit for the Party: whether it's securing ballot access, organizing precincts, online advocacy, phone banking, or financial contributions. Party members also need to be willing to support the party's candidates. We have to be proactive rather than expect the perfect candidate to pop in and give us someone to unite around.

History has critical lessons for those who base their party around a single leader. When the Constitution Party was founded as the U.S. Taxpayers Party, it hoped Pat Buchanan would agree to be their standard bearer after his failed but strong Republican primary campaigns. To make things convenient for Buchanan, the U.S. Taxpayers Party held their 1996 convention in San Diego after the Republican Convention in the same city, so Buchanan could walk out from the GOP convention and accept the U.S. Taxpayers Party nomination.

Buchanan did eventually run as a third-party candidate, in 2000…for the Reform Party. The Taxpayers Party efforts to woo Buchanan were wasted. The Taxpayers Party would have done better to make itself a competitive political presence, something it has yet to do to this day despite its name change.

The Reform Party offers a lesson of its own. Ross Perot's 19% of the vote is the highest total by any third-party candidate since 1912. For his pro-government reform movement to have a chance, it needed to result in the formation of a national party. That's why he started the Reform Party and ran on its national ticket. He only got 8% of the vote in his second run, but that qualified the Reform Party for $20 million in federal matching funds in the 2000 election. This would put whoever they nominated at a great advantage.

Unfortunately, not enough Reform Party members got involved in the state and local parties. This led to outsiders coming in to take over state party organizations and secure the nomination. Perot represented a reform-centric, moderate position on the issues. The fight for the Reform Party nomination came down to the right-wing nationalist Pat Buchanan and the transcendental meditation advocate John Hagelin, who'd run twice before on the Natural Law Party ticket. Buchanan formed a strange alliance with Marxist Lenora Fulani in a game that could be best categorized as *Win Ross Perot's Money.*

Buchanan won the nomination but in the general, he won less than half a percent of the vote, signaling the Reform Party's end as a political force.

The Reform party's collapse is a reminder political parties need to not be just concerned with a strong performance in the Presidential race. Parties need to be healthy from the ground up, so success doesn't merely invite political vultures to pick apart the party's body.

A successful party will build an organization that will allow its members to run for state and local office and that will attract good candidates. These are the people who a party wants to come.

Some skilled political figures from the major parties should be welcomed. However, a new political party's goal should be to groom its own members to serve in offices at the state and local levels and to become the party's future candidates for national office. By creating a party infrastructure that will allow successful campaigns, a new political party will attract the type of leaders that it wants and that America so desperately needs.

Part II

How to Establish a New Party

Chapter 10
Building a New Coalition

Any third party on the right faces one key argument that dissuades many. It's a compelling and logical argument. It's not an ideological argument but a mathematical one.

It's simply stated, "In a closely divided country, if you establish a third party or run as an Independent Candidate, all you'll end up doing is splitting the vote Republicans get and ensuring a Democrat wins whatever elections you compete in."

First, third-party candidates' effect is overstated as an excuse for failed major party candidates. For example, in 1992, George H.W. Bush violated his "no new taxes" pledge and admitted he struggled with "the vision thing." That is why he only got 38% of the vote. It's convenient for Republicans to blame Ross Perot.

In 2000, the Clinton/Gore administration took the country so far to the left, Al Gore lost Clinton's home state of Arkansas and Tennessee, the state Gore represented in the Senate for eight years. However, many allege Ralph Nader's Green Party cost Gore Florida by Nader garnering less than three percent of the vote.

In a 2015 piece in the American Spectator, Bill Pascoe examined the myth Perot caused Bush's defeat. Pascoe noted Bush was widely unpopular. During a three-month period in which Perot was out of the Presidential race, Bush never led in the polls. Once Perot got back in, Perot picked up thirteen points.

Says Pascoe, "In other words, to the extent voters left Bush and Clinton for Perot, those who left Clinton for Perot outnumbered those who left Bush for Perot by more than 4-to-1." The New York Times in 1992 reported exit polls showed Perot's voters would have split 38-38% had he not been in the race, with 24% not voting at all.

In 2000, CNN's exit poll showed George W. Bush winning the vital state of Florida by two percentage points had Nader not been in the race.

It is one thing to say major party candidates are responsible for their own wins and losses and another to say you can build a third-party that can win. You can't do that by drawing members from just Republicans. If the country is split 50-50, a new party that drew its members from only one side will tip the balance to the other side.

Most third parties have been designed with the goal of serving the people who started it. The Libertarian Party and Constitution Party exist to advocate a particular viewpoint and cater strictly to the people who hold it. A new party will start with key principles but it will not be a place where ideologues debate how many angels dance on the head of a pin.

We need to step back a bit and look at the big picture of America. The left-right political divide is between activists and other passionate participants in the political process. For most Americans, politics does not drive them.

When you are a political activist, some numbers will amaze you. When exit polls show some self-identified conservatives voted for Hillary Clinton or a percentage of self-identified liberals voted for Donald Trump, it puzzles you because voting that way doesn't make sense to you.

Political activists and conservatives are bedeviled by what authors Chip and Dan Heath call the Curse of Knowledge. When you know something, it is difficult to imagine not knowing it.

When you are active in a political party, read political publications, and wade into the cesspool of Internet political debate regularly, you may primarily identify with a political tribe. Most Americans don't. Their tribe is their literal ethnic group, religion, occupation, or lifestyle-based identity group. Whatever their tribe is, it is not a political party. Their political beliefs are flexible. Their prejudices and biases are based on limited information. And their opinion of both major parties is not positive.

We can reach out to these people to build something new, different, and better in American politics. Once we are unbound from the tired politics of the past and the GOP's toxic brand, there is an opportunity for conservatives to build a positive and hopeful party that will bring a wide swath of Americans together in a new coalition.

This quest's beginning is the wide swath of disaffected voters and non-voters. Of those eligible to vote, 40% did not vote. In addition, some who vote take a hot shower afterward, due to the disgust they feel with their choices.

Younger evangelicals are a key target demographic. We're less likely than our elders to buy into Trump's lies and line up to defend him. Most of us still believe character is important in public servants even while our elders cast both concepts aside in favor of strong men owed blind loyalty reigning over us. Quite a few evangelicals under forty are politically astute and conservative, albeit most of us are not big on politics.

Right-of-center women disenchanted by Donald Trump's mistreatment of women would also be a key group for a new party to engage with.

When it comes to reaching outside the typical GOP base, a new party will also reach out to Democratic voters, particularly minority voters and those who live in urban areas, where the GOP outreach is often non-existent. In the following chapters, we'll examine some of the elements of this new coalition.

Chapter 11
Boldly Going Where Conservatives Haven't Gone Before

Racial reconciliation and conservative outreach to minorities are ideas that have inspired numerous books and articles. I won't attempt to cover the subject exhaustively. Rather, I will offer a few observations on the way things stand in 2018 in regards to how a new political party needs to approach this sensitive issue.

It would be a mistake to assume a new party could completely dodge the bad will caused by the Republicans' many mistakes over the years. We certainly will not if we continue to act as the Republicans have acted.

First and foremost, we must all come to an understanding that, in all ethnic groups, there exists both people of good will and people of bad will. The people of bad will deserve a special focus.

Some white political leaders' stock and trade is stirring up resentment and fear among whites towards minorities. They turn issues like illegal immigration and racial preferences and quotas into a pretext for divisive racial messages and their politics of resentment and fear. They speak using "dog whistles," phrases unwary listeners will not pick up on, but which resonate with their audience of white separatists and white supremacists. When challenged by good people in the know, they give a "who me?" smile, deny their racist subtext, and soon repeat their talking points and its racist subtext.

Some minority leaders' lives center around sustaining racial resentment. They turn scenes of tragedies into media circuses about them and their message rather than about the people who are suffering. They stir up and thrive on racial animosity and mistrust. Sometimes, their efforts are born out of self-promotion or a desire to raise funds for their organizations. Others use racial resentment to draw people into a more radical intersectional movement.

Whatever their angle is, people of bad will do not want racial harmony. They benefit from the racial angst and infighting and want it to continue indefinitely, because they thrive on it.

People of good will seek to know their own prejudices, overcome them, treat others with respect regardless of their differences. Though imperfect, they strive to be decent, caring people. It is people of good will of all racial and ethnic backgrounds that a new party should seek to reach.

Reaching them doesn't require we abandon conservative principles. It does require we show sense, tact, flexibility, and empathy, at least more than the Republicans have shown in the past.

Take for example the Black Lives Matter (BLM) movement. The BLM organization takes a hard-line against America's police forces. Ron Hosko, writing in the Hill on October 12, 2016, detailed the number of people signing up to become policemen has plummeted due to the activity of Black Lives Matter. The organization's rallies include vile chants like, "Pigs in a blanket, fry 'em like bacon!" and "What do we want? Dead cops! When do we want them? Now!"

The Black Lives Matter protests have led to timid policing methods in the City of Baltimore. The results? A record high number of blacks murdered in 2017.

In an interview with NPR, Kinji Scott, an African-American minister from the Baltimore area said, "It pisses me off when people keep talking about reform," he says. "We're talking about our safety and being able to walk out of our houses without being shot."

Beyond the tragedy of BLM-backed policies leading to more black lives destroyed, the group has a radical agenda far beyond racial issues. The group has a presence with Democratic Socialists of America. In an interview with the LA Times, BLM founder Patrisse Cullors put "capitalism" amongst her list of the evils of America on the level of racism. In an article for the Foundation for Economic Education, Marian Tupy notes that the U.K. version of BLM was founded by a representative of the Socialist Workers Party.

Much about the BLM organization's activities deserves to be challenged and opposed. However, conservative critiques often attack people who simply resonate with the phrase "Black lives matter" and have no connection to the organization called that. They often know little to nothing about the BLM group's agenda.

Conservatives have to show understanding for why that idea resonates with blacks. The sad fact is many believe that their lives don't matter to the majority of Americans, certainly not as much as the lives of white people. Their sincere feeling is, "Hey, our lives matter, too." Not "Black lives matter more than cop lives, the cops are the enemy, kill them and end capitalism!"

It's not just liberals who tells us this. Few senators are as conservative as Senator Tim Scott (R-SC), the first Black American elected to the Senate from the South since reconstruction. In a 2016 speech to the U.S. Senate, Scott said he was pulled over seven times in a single year while serving in Congress. Most of the time, it was for driving a nice car in the wrong neighborhood.

A black member of Scott's staff traded in for a cheaper car because he got stopped so many times by the Washington, DC police. Scott was also confronted by a Capitol Policeman and required to show his ID despite the fact he was wearing his U.S. Senate pin, which is the only identification of that every other member of that body is required to produce.

Yet Scott's speech was mostly ignored by those who pretend there are no racism problems among police officers. Many white conservatives put cops on a hero's pedestal, assume anyone killed by a cop is guilty of actions justifying it, and refuse to hear or respect the reasons that anyone has to harbor suspicions a police shooting is unjustified and racially motivated.

Many other evils also cause black Americans to question whether their lives matter to mainstream America. There's the phenomena noted by the late Gwen Ifil known as Missing White Woman syndrome. If a missing person is young, beautiful, blonde, and white, she can garner national media coverage. When minority women and children vanish in comparable situations, they are barely mentioned, if they are covered at all.

In addition, many black men have found themselves the targets of false accusations meant to cover for other people's crimes. Back in 1994, Susan Smith let her car roll into a lake, killing her two sons, aged three and fourteen months. To cover up the crime, she falsely claimed a black man carjacked her and kidnapped the two boys.

In a New York Times piece from November 6, 1994, a black security guard said, "I guess she figured if she said a black man did it people would believe her no matter what kind of story she came up with. That's what hurts. As long as it's allegedly a black man involved, America will fall for anything."

The same Times story reported, five years before in Boston, a white man claimed a black man shot his pregnant wife when the husband had done it. Boston Police questioned numerous black men and even arrested one before the truth came out and the real killer committed suicide.

Much progress has been made for racial minorities and women in the past few decades, but this doesn't mean all the problems have been solved. It's important to acknowledge that and seek to empathize with these problems.

This doesn't mean a new party should embrace leftist narratives of race that define people as helpless victims in constant need of government help. And we certainly should not cast all police officers as racists or adopt the failed policies of the left.

We need to avoid the mistakes of many on the left who label people of good will as "racists" and tell those who don't agree with popular narratives to "check their privilege." The left calls it a privilege to have basic human rights respected (dangerous, given that privileges can be lawfully revoked) and uses "check your privilege" to shut down conversation.

However, a new party can't put on blinders, pretend all issues with racism have been resolved, and expect to win over members of minority community who face significant, real problems.

In few cases would a change in government policy be helpful. Far many more require a change in cultural attitudes. It's important for conservatives to recognize this. Conservatives would be fools to get into a contest over who wants the most government programs to solve problems. We should advocate solutions in accordance with our principles.

Some readers will complain I'm calling for conservatives to be "politically correct." If that means not being a prejudiced bully, why, yes, I am. However, it doesn't. It means a stifling list of man-made rules that liberals try to impose. This leads to ridiculous verbal gymnastics or laughable violence to the English language such as when Canadian Prime Minister corrected a woman for using, "Mankind" and informed her the correct term was "people kind."

Yet, in the age of Trump, "not being politically correct," has become an excuse for treating people with contempt and lacking concern for their welfare. That needs to stop if we want to win over minorities to the conservative cause. We need to show some consideration for them.

We need to make our arguments with respect. Racial preferences and set asides are wrong because they discriminate against whites and are patronizing to minorities. But don't spread the message, "you don't have a job because a minority got it." Before posting a diatribe against illegal immigration, be sure you don't come across as anti-Hispanic.

Within our own coalition, conservatives manage to show respect and decency in the way we approach others all the time. Irreligious libertarians don't all sound like anti-Christian bigots like Bill Maher. Catholics, Protestants, and members of the LDS faith operate within the same coalitions by showing each other respect despite wide theological and cultural differences. Are they being politically correct or are they showing owed sensitivity and decency?

It is not a huge challenge to extend this to minority voters. If a new party refuses to do that, it will never capture a significant portion of that vote.

While respecting minorities is a pre-requisite for success in America's urban centers, it doesn't guarantee it. More work is required. The Republicans have abandoned most major cities. Its platform and its policies are focused on America's rural and suburban populations. Even in Suburbia, the GOP is in decline. Democrats have run most major cities for decades with no substantive opposition, leading to deepening poverty and corruption.

This creates a great opportunity for a new party to step in to offer alternatives to the failed big government agenda of the Democrats. Challenges to over-regulation and corruption, along with issues such as school and creating economic opportunity, could serve as a basis for building a successful opposition party in major cities.

The challenge will be that cities are unlikely to yield results to a new party any time soon. However, when building state parties, it is crucial to develop a greater presence and focus in urban centers. This will ensure the party does more than take votes away from the Republicans. In addition, the greater the number of votes won in urban areas, the greater chance the party will have of winning statewide elections.

Chapter 12
Red Hat People and a New Party

On the Internet, it's easy to see the worst people and assume they represent their entire identity group. This is certainly true with Trump supporters: Racists march in the street, angry mobs fill rallies, and the legions of ignorant Internet trolls get the anti-Trump folks into a self-righteous furor about never having anything to do with Trump supporters.

Yet that's not all Trump supporters. Some people back Trump without being racists or fanatics sold on lies. As we've discussed in previous chapters, Washington's Republican leadership let people down and there's ample reason to be upset. Some support Trump out of fear of the Democrats, who certainly are no better.

Some anti-Trumpers can't believe any decent person could back Trump, but as National Review writer David French has said this view overestimates the degree to which Trump supporters know of Trump's flaws and the degree to which they believe them.

In addition, the distrust of opposition media has limited some people's information. There are facts you don't get by watching Fox News. Even if you indulge in a bit of mainstream media, Trump plays them so well, they flit from one controversy to another, unable to focus on what Trump did wrong that's important.

There is a cult of personality behind Trump, but political cult members can eventually come to their senses. Take Peggy Joseph, a woman interviewed at an Obama rally in 2008 who said, "I won't have to worry about putting gas in my car, I won't have to worry about paying my mortgage! If I help him, he's going to help me!" She became a symbol of the exuberant hopes raised in the Obama cult of personality. By 2014, as reported by the Washington Times, Joseph had a change of heart, admitting she'd gotten caught up in the excitement of the first Black presidential candidate.

Time and distance led her to compare Obama to the Wizard of Oz, calling him, "The little man behind the curtain, not who we thought or expected him to be."

Hopefully, in time, many conservatives will have that awakening with Trump. A new party won't cater to the conspiracy theorists, racists, or cranks. However, if a party wants to build a successful coalition, it would do well how to figure out how to reach out to the some of the people who support Trump.

Here are three quick guidelines that should be considered:

Seek Genuine Candidates

The one thing I can say for Donald Trump is he's a unique person. His re-actions, life story, and experiences are not the typical ones for politicians. While so much about his persona and his claims are exaggerated or downright lies, he's certainly original.

You can't say that about most political leaders, particularly Republicans. As Amanda Carpenter wrote in her book *Gaslighting America,* the type of the people the GOP embraced for high office tended to be very similar. They have similar backgrounds, almost identical ways of addressing issues, and even dress as if they came off a factory assembly line.

Those who didn't fit into the mold would get shoved into the mold under the tutelage of other leaders. The mold just screamed inauthenticity.

Without compromising on issues of character and integrity, a new party needs to seek authentic leaders who can be themselves without being offensive or boorish. It needs people with a variety of life experiences and approaches to the political process rather than producing leaders whose similarity to each other makes them seem robotic.

Address the Concerns of Ordinary People, Particularly on Safety

Too often, Republican and conservative leaders have gotten into the trap of spending all of their time addressing issues only of concern to ideologue donors. A new party has to address the concerns of average voters.

It's important to not fall into the trap of being too politically correct to address hot button issues that concern voters. Trump is lauded for daring to address issues like illegal immigration. He deserves criticism for addressing it with demagoguery, sowing racial fear and distrust, and setting America further back from uniting around a fair solution, but he does raise the issue.

As I wrote in the previous chapter, a new party can't address immigration in a way that comes off as anti-Hispanic. It also can't afford to address the issue with the assumption that anyone who has concerns with illegal immigration is racist.

Many debates over immigration and the incendiary statements about it miss the point for most voters. For example, President Trump unfairly accuses all Mexican immigrants of being violent criminals, claiming that illegal aliens commit crimes at a higher rate than the U.S. citizens born to Americans. He's wrong to paint all illegal immigrants as monsters. Truth is, illegal immigrants are not more likely to be incarcerated and may be less likely.

However, the evil racial hatred Trump incites doesn't justify reacting to it by ignoring any genuine threats to public safety. Citing statistics on low crime rates among illegal aliens won't heal a family whose child was raped and killed. If individuals are in the U.S. illegally, they do commit crimes here, and they are released or lost in the bureaucracy and they do kill someone, that's a consequence of our failure to protect our border and enforce the laws.

Lax public safety policies do no service to vulnerable immigrants, legal or otherwise. That is another lesson to learn from Baltimore, where soft public safety policies intended to protect black lives instead put them more at risk than ever.

Similarly, the idea illegal immigrants come to the country for welfare is false and unfair. Most come here to work hard, earn a living, and give charity to relatives living in abject poverty. At the same time, illegal immigrants can become a drain on taxpayer resources through the need to access government health services or education for children. Screaming "racist!" and ignoring the reasonable concerns around border security drives people to back demagogues who will at least talk about the issue.

Many people want increased legal immigration, a guest worker program, and they want a resolution for those already here illegally. None of these goals are without merit, but they will all fail as a matter of course until the nation's borders are secure.

People deserve to feel their families and their country are safe. Politicians have promised to secure the border later in exchange for passing amnesty now but they have failed to deliver, most notably the immigration amnesty during the Reagan Administration. This has created a trust deficit with conservative voters. The only way to bridge that trust deficit is to secure the border.

In addition, immigration needs to be controlled along with our borders. Note that's not closed or open. Controlled borders are practical. If everyone who wanted to come to America came here, how soon would America have a population of one billion people? How would our schools and social safety net support that high of infusion of people?

We are not prepared for a population surge, so our immigration needs to be managed. A new party will take a reasonable approach and establish healthy national boundaries that are fair to all and compassionate. It will not embrace nonsense like The Wall, which is an extravagant real estate scheme concocted by a man who made a fortune selling extravagant real estate schemes.

Still, America needs to take border security seriously. In many spots on the border, fencing, sometimes double and triple fencing, has been effective deterrents to illegal crossings. More parts of the border could benefit. Getting wider use of e-verify by employers and addressing the Visa Overstays and the problem of sanctuary cities will do a lot to relieve stress on the border.

When the public feels safer, there will be more latitude to make reasonable changes in our immigration system. Legal immigration is vital to America's future. Importing more workers may be one way we can mitigate the coming crisis in our Social Security and Medicare system caused by a declining worker to retiree ratio. However, for positive changes to occur, first the people need to feel that the government is keeping them and their families secure.

Stand for True Patriotism

President Trump takes advantage of patriotic symbolism. Patriotic motifs dominate his rallies and he has wrapped his re-election campaign in the American flag. He has taken the issue of NFL protests of the National Anthem and made it a keystone of his culture war rallying point.

Under President Obama, patriotism was downplayed. The extreme left thinks little of America's symbols and heritage to begin with and has become even less comfortable with patriotic symbols and rhetoric thanks to Trump's use of patriotic symbols.

This discomfort can be seen in the movie *First Man,* a biopic about Neil Armstrong that will not include planting the American flag on the Moon. New York Governor Andrew Cuomo (D-NY)'s response to President Trump's famous slogan was, "American was never that great." Cuomo walked back the statement but many far leftists strongly defended it.

A new party needs to remember that some patriotism can be good. Loving your country, honoring the heroes who built it, and celebrating its symbols and culture is healthy and key to national unity. This doesn't mean we put on blinders to the faults of our nation's heroes. It means we respect what they did for our country in spite of their acknowledged faults. A new political party will celebrate what is truly good about America.

Most people want to feel good about their nation, not have it torn down all the time. That said, a new party will offer a better patriotism than President Trump offers.

While President Trump uses patriotic symbolism often, there's little true patriotism behind it. President Trump has little understanding of the Constitution and the limits on his executive power. He disrespects the Bill of Rights. He has often made the Kremlin's case for the moral equivalence between our country and the murderous regime of Vladimir Putin.

Behind President Trump's patriotic packaging is a toxic brand of nationalism. Nationalism is the fool's gold of patriotism. True patriotism is based on love of your country, its history, and its symbolism. President Trump's nationalism is based upon fear and loathing of the outsider and insecurity about our ability to compete and survive in a diverse world.

A new party's patriotism will have substance behind it beyond just celebrating the flag and the anthem. It will celebrate the Constitution and the Bill of Rights. It will recognize all America has done that is truly great. For example, defeating Fascism in World War II, fighting Communism and liberating millions in the Cold War, and saving millions from the scourge of AIDS. True patriotism also celebrates everyone who has come to this country from other lands to make their lives better and have enriched us all in the process.

In 1946, President Truman signed a proclamation designating September 17 as "I Am An American Day" to celebrate "all who, by coming of age or naturalization, have attained the status of citizenship." The day became Citizenship Day, and was combined with Constitution Day, and has fallen out of popular use. A new party could lead the way in bringing Citizenship Day back.

Let's hold celebrations to honor those hard-working immigrants who've completed the legal requirements to become citizens and all the young people who've reached voting age. Let's embrace law-abiding immigrants without fear—in an orderly fashion—and celebrate all new citizens along with young voters. A new party will represent a healthy patriotism, which is open-hearted and not based upon fear.

Chapter 13
Foundation For a New Party #1:
Consistent Constitutionalism

A new party must represent certain principles. Many will be hashed out when the party writes its platform. We'll address writing the party platform in future chapters. However, a new party needs to have foundational principles in response to the abuses of the major parties. This will help ensure the party will be a positive force in the country. Some of these principles may end up getting written into the platform, but they are more fundamental that. They are operating principles that are non-negotiable.

America's major parties are both inconsistent and hypocritical in almost every area of our national life. For example, take the confirmation of judges. It used to be, to confirm any judge required the passage of a cloture motion by sixty members of the Senate to end debate. In the mid-2000s, Senate Democrats filibustered George W Bush's judicial nominees. Conservatives grew frustrated and pushed for a "nuclear option" to end it. This dubious process would allow fifty-one Senators to change the rules of the Senate.

A bi-partisan group of fourteen senators came together to thwart this effort. This "gang of fourteen" also sought to curtail filibusters another way. Yet the Republican members of the gang of fourteen were reproached as traitors. Two were defeated for re-election. Eight years later, Republicans filibustered President Obama's judicial nominees and executive appointees. To end this, Democratic Senate Majority Leader Harry Reid used the nuclear option. The right was furious at Reid's "dictatorial" move, and the left praised it.

In 2017, Senate Majority Leader Mitch McConnell (R-KY) used the nuclear option with Supreme Court nominees. The same Democrats who praised Reid for it attacked McConnell for it. The Republicans furious at Reid likewise praised McConnell.

Next take the issue of spending. Republicans have forgotten all concerns about the national debt and profligate spending that were front and center now that Trump is in the White House.

In all of this, no real principle was at stake, only the question of whose ox gets gored. What were once sacrosanct ideals are now matters of convenience and situational ethics. For our country to survive as a free nation, we must do better than this.

America's Constitutional system is remarkable. Its wise systems of checks and balances has kept our nation a free republic for more than 225 years. It is also a frustrating system for those who want quick political change. Massive political changes are not easily achieved and that is by design. The Founders recognized a system subject to quick, violent changes would not be sustainable and would not be free.

For many ideologues, the Constitution can be sacrificed to achieve their goals. Most of the left's victories on social issues has not come from persuading their fellow citizens of the wisdom of their position. Instead, the left has enacted change by turning to the courts. Were courts taking a look at the plain text of the Constitution and ruling by it, this would not be a problem. That's not what's been going on.

The judicial branch has been demeaning itself for decades by acting like lawmakers. Judges across the country embrace the "living Constitution" theory. This allows them to read into the Constitution things never intended by its authors. The Supreme Court is willing to serve as a Constitutional Convention, declaring new rights of their own invention.

To bypass the ballot box, the left gets five Supreme Court justices to create new rights and new protected classes out of the ether. They proclaim their edits are sacred and as much a part of the Constitution as if it had been drafted in Philadelphia in 1787. Those on the other side of this debate know this is a lie and these tactics leave lingering resentments that deepen our divisions.

At the same time, the power of the Executive Branch has grown beyond all bounds. Too many Presidents have governed by executive orders, effectively bypassing the legislative branch and making law through executive fiat.

Presidents have also abused the Constitution's recess appointment provision to temporarily fill vacant government posts while Congress is out of session. This power was given in the eighteenth century. Then, the Senate was out of session half of the year and transportation was slow. Presidents abuse this provision to put in office nominees that the Senate won't confirm. To avoid this, the Senate Majority Leader often won't officially recess the Senate.

In addition, consider the federal departments and agencies. They should issue guidelines for following federal laws. Instead they effectively pass new laws, without congress's accountability to the American people.

Overstepping Constitutional power limits enraptures partisans in power. It enrages the same partisans when they're not in power.

With so many abuses of power, it's important to ask what's happened to the legislative branch as the ultimate lawmaking power. Members of Congress have fallen down on the job. The current national situation lets Congress avoid tough political decisions. If an agency or a court decides on some hot topic, then Congress doesn't have to answer to the voters for it. This leaves time for members of Congress to do what they do best: posture.

The New York Times quotes National Review Columnist Jonah Goldberg as saying, "It's not so much a Congress as much as it has become a parliament of pundits. Everyone just wants to secure their position on 'Morning Joe' or 'Fox & Friends.'"

We need more than a new President. We need a new Congress that will stand up and re-assert its constitutional prerogatives. We need a new political party that will stand consistently for the Constitutional order.

We have to maintain the proper limits and roles of the federal government to remain a free people. Many leaders have failed to stay within their Constitutional limits. This has undermined the American people's faith in their form of government.

Such overreaches have to be checked, whatever form they may take.

Respect for the Constitution doesn't bar us from any support for changing it. The Framers did not believe their work was inalterable and could last forever without amendment. They knew challenges would arise. They made provision for amendments and for another Convention of the States drafting a new constitution. However, we must not change the Constitution by judicial or executive fiat, or by ignoring its provisions. Rather change must come through the processes that the Founders laid out.

Chapter 14
Foundation for a New Party #2:
Character and Ethics

In 2011, in a Brookings Institute survey, 30% of Evangelical Christians deemed private unethical behavior irrelevant to a politician's job performance. That number jumped to 72% as Evangelicals changed their position to support Donald Trump for President. Catholics and Mainline Protestants also underwent jumps to this position, though less pronounced.

One religious argument for abandoning all concerns about character is Trump was not running for pastor. Have we considered all of the implications of this? Do we truly want to live in a country where we only expect the clergy to have good morals, ethics, or decency? We've taken "don't judge" to such an extreme, we can't call out unethical behavior in anyone but the clergy. From school teachers to bank employees to small business owners to the President.

If we remain the sort of country we've become, we cannot long sustain liberty. As John Adams wrote in 1798, "We have no Government armed with Power capable of contending with human Passions unbridled by morality and Religion. Avarice, Ambition Revenge or Gallantry, would break the strongest Cords of our Constitution as a Whale goes through a Net. Our Constitution was made only for a moral and religious People."

The right is far from the only side that has been inconsistent on the character issue. We've seen the left show concerns about Donald Trump's sex life they never showed about Bill Clinton. Even when Clinton was credibly accused of sexual assault or rape.

Clinton's sexual misconduct and Obama's breaches of Presidential protocol and democratic norms have been cited as defenses of Trump's behavior. This poison is a logical fallacy popularly called whataboutism. There's no real attempt to justify the conduct, only to show the hypocrisy of the person calling out the misconduct. This doesn't work so well on conservative Trump critics. Many a Trump backer will try to attack us with, "You liberals didn't say anything when Obama did this." However, we are conservatives, we did call out Obama, too, and we are being consistent.

Whataboutism surrenders moral high ground and lowers the bar for our elected officials. What Republicans let Trump get away with, the next leftwing President will get away with. What Democrats let the next leftwing President get away with, the next rightwing President will get away with. Whataboutism creates a downward spiral. It leads to less ethics, more abandonment of American principles, and more government abuse of America's citizens

We need to be consistent in demanding leaders of good character and in insisting on ethical conduct while in office. The main indicator we have of how faithfully our leaders will perform their public duties is how they honor their private ones. A man unfaithful to his wife will also be unfaithful to his constituents and to his country. It is important to take a broad view of character and not limit our concern to only fidelity in marriage, though. We should ask how they treat other people in their lives.

Even had Donald Trump been innocent of any sexual wrongdoing, his business practices are a character issue. He used his power as a wealthy person to cheat business partners, contractors, and many others. This should've been enough to persuade Americans not to give him power. Dishonest people who abuse the weak in the private sector will also do so in the public sector.

A new party should be concerned with the character of the candidates it nominates. If its candidates are as corrupt as the major party candidates, they will not succeed.

However, it's important to balance the desire for leaders of good moral character with an understanding of human frailty and weakness. If we demand morally perfect candidates, no one interested in running will qualify. We are all flawed and we have all made mistakes. We have to use good judgment to determine whether a personal failing is both persistent and severe enough to be disqualifying.

First, resolved issues from long ago are irrelevant to who a candidate is today. In his autobiography Standing Firm, former Vice-President Dan Quayle stated he was nervous when he was under consideration for Vice-President in 1988. Why? An FBI background check could uncover a time he'd been publicly drunk in college.

Youthful indiscretions a candidate that has outgrown are not of concern. People mature over time. George W. Bush's statement, "When I was young and irresponsible, I was young and irresponsible," covers a lot of ground. Having been a stupid youth over two decades prior to running for office shouldn't disqualify a now-wiser adult for office.

Even when someone failed in the past as a full-grown adult, their failing should be considered in light of any mitigating circumstances and their behavior in the time since then. If a sixty-year-old cheated on his wife and ruined his marriage twenty years ago, he shouldn't be forever disqualified. Nor should the passage of time automatically absolve him. What matters is if he's admitted his wrongs, accepted the consequences, and changed his ways.

A discerning voter is concerned with who the candidates are now. If their lives reflect that they have learned from their errors and become better people, then we should be willing to support them. On the other hand, if their behavior twenty years ago is part of a pattern that continues to this day, then a wise voter won't trust such candidates.

When we are evaluating a candidate's character, the issue is trust. Evangelical supporters of President Trump think the issue is forgiveness and accuse opponents of not forgiving Trump. The truth is, the majority of us have nothing to forgive. Unless you're a woman he mistreated or one of the people he conned, Trump's wrongs are not against you, and it's not your place to forgive Trump. Even when it is, it is possible to forgive someone and to conclude the person is not trustworthy.

The issue for voters isn't whether we should forgive political leaders but whether we can trust political leaders.

That said, we should avoid rejecting trustworthy candidates of a different faith or identity group. We should not hold candidates to sectarian total prohibitions on alcohol or tobacco use. If their lives generally show good character, clear-headed judgment, and they support the new party's platform and agenda, then let that be sufficient.

Once they are elected to office, we should demand high ethical standards from our leaders. I've documented the hypocrisy of both parties in chapters two, three, and six. But respect for political integrity also requires a proper respect for the impeachment and ethics processes.

The partisans in both political parties go to extremes on these issues. Partisans who don't hold the presidency begin calling for impeachment before the new President takes office. They'll offer no impeachable offense. They demand investigations of things with no evidence that warrants an investigation. Many partisans file frivolous complaints to hurt politicians on the other side.

Partisans in power will refuse to impeach under any circumstances. They ignore ethical breaches they would scream bloody murder about if they weren't in power. When a party holds the Presidency and Congressional oversight, partisans use committees to whitewash unpleasant issues.

To an extent, the behavior of the partisans out of power drives the action of the in-power partisans. This could be seen in the Clinton impeachment. Part of the reason many Democrats were not inclined to support impeachment is many on the right were trying to impeach Clinton going back to 1993. To support impeachment even after he had committed perjury and obstructed justice would be letting the GOP win. For the same reason, the GOP won't consider impeaching President Trump regardless of what evidence is found against him.

If they hold the Presidency, partisans will invest themselves heavily in defending the President. They psychologically need to be right about him and his policies and to condemn the other side. This combination of pride and partisan hatred blinds them to the President's corruption. No matter how much evidence of corruption piles up, it is all deemed enemy lies.

Voters are cynical about processes that need credibility to hold the government accountable. On social media, partisans share congressional hearing clips that "destroy" their opponents. How much does the general public care? Most know Congressional investigative hearings are about grandstanding and gamesmanship. If the truth comes out, it is incidental to winning.

A new party must be consistently principled in its support for ethics in government and must address corruption in a non-partisan way. Partisanship has created a toxic environment where politicians can get away with anything.

This is far too dangerous. While preparing for the Senate Impeachment trial of Bill Clinton in 1999, the chief house manager Rep. Henry Hyde (R-IL) plead for more time and more witnesses. He shared a lot of evidence had not been made public due to the rush by House leaders to impeach Clinton. Senator Ted Stevens (R-AK) informed Hyde sixty-seven Senators would not vote to remove Clinton even if the evidence proved Clinton had raped and killed a woman. In 2015, while still a candidate, President Trump boasted he could shoot someone on Fifth Avenue in New York and not lose any support for it.

Stevens was right about Clinton, and Trump was right about himself.

Thankfully, Trump hasn't committed murder, and there's also no evidence Clinton has, either. Yet, due to the number of blind partisans on both sides, either one of them could have gotten away with it while in office.

Around the world, bad political leaders get away with murder, often on a regular basis. A civilization that tolerates corruption in high officials is headed down this dangerous road. A new party must be better. We need to be citizens before we're partisans. A partisan will view saving a corrupt official as a win over the other side. A citizen will view fighting for a government free of corruption as in all of our best interests.

We need to reject political cults of personality. We need open eyes and a clear head when we think about individual political leaders. Remember we do not know these people beyond their public persona and our best guess of who they are based on what we see. Most public personas are masks worn by the "private" person, and our guesses of who that person is may be wrong.

Politicians should be treated like fruit and thrown out if they're rotten. No political leader should be viewed as irreplaceable or essential. No politician is worth leading our nation down the road to becoming a banana republic.

At the same time, the integrity of processes to hold politicians accountable should not be compromised for partisan gains. A new party will reject attempts to use impeachment as a means to overturn election results they don't like. A new party should stand against the use of frivolous ethics complaints against political leaders as a partisan tactic.

Note that tactic isn't good statesmanship or good politics. Far more politicians survive ethics investigations than are taken down by them. When a politician is caught in a scandal, it often does lead to another party claiming that politician's office. The time spent prosecuting opponents detracts from the party's overall mission to convince voters you care about them, have plans to address their issues, and implement those plans.

A new party needs to recognize voters have grown cynical with political parties trying to prosecute their way into power. Ethics proceedings like impeachment are extraordinary measures. They should be used when there is evidence of a serious crime or ethics violation. It's wise to not comment on allegations against political foes until the investigations are complete. When an opponent wins an election, the party's strategy should assume the next opportunity to replace them will come at the next election.

A new party needs to be proactive with its own leaders. It shouldn't rush to judgment since there have been many false charges, but unwavering defenses are ill-advised. A party should use some wisdom in determining the seriousness of the offense. We should not require superhuman perfection of our leaders, and not every failing requires ending a political career.

However, if it becomes clear a candidate or official is corrupt, their own party must have the strongest voices calling for their removal. This is not easy. When you're in the same party, relationships are formed. However hard it is, it still must be done. To have merit, a new party must seek to restore ethics and integrity to our political process at any personal cost.

Chapter 15
Foundations for a New Party #3:
Consistent Support for the First Amendment

In the movie *Mister Smith Goes to Washington,* Senator Jeff Smith (played by Jimmy Stewart) says, "I'm free to think and to speak. My ancestors couldn't. I can. And my children will." This shows a profound respect for the freedoms American citizens enjoy that today is often considered cheesy. However, we would be wise to appreciate our freedoms and understand they are fragile.

Sadly, many Americans are ignorant of their First Amendment rights. According to a 2017 Annenberg Public Policy Institute poll, thirty-seven percent of American's can't name any of the rights guaranteed under the First Amendment. Yet the words of our First Amendment recognize the key liberties many Americans take for granted. "Congress shall make no law respecting an establishment of religion, or prohibiting the free exercise thereof; or abridging the freedom of speech, or of the press; or the right of the people peaceably to assemble, and to petition the Government for a redress of grievances."

Freedom of religion, freedom of speech, freedom of the press are revocable, rare privileges on most of Earth. Tens of millions are persecuted for their faiths around the world. In countless countries, religious dissidents can be executed on blasphemy charges.

Restrictions on free speech abound all around the world. This ranges from the iron-fisted control China exercises over what its people believe to the less severe speech code commissions around the world that put ministers, news columnists, and others who defy the speech code through a mockery of justice.

Americans have their choice of information sources. Around the world, the press is often a propaganda arm of the state. For example, Vladimir Putin's Russia. Those who report news the government doesn't want to get out face constant danger. According to the Canadian Broadcasting Company, eighty-one professional journalists were killed in 2017.

The freedoms guaranteed by America's First Amendment are a rich heritage, yet these freedoms are under attack from both major parties. The Democrats and the Republicans both only believe in these freedoms whey they advance their own causes. For America to remain free, these freedoms must be respected at all times. Even when it's inconvenient and unhelpful.

Freedom of Religion may be the most powerful good that holds our nation together. Our Founders were descended from men who came to Europe. The history of Europe at that point was of religious sects taking turns persecuting each other. The First Amendment bars the government of the United States from oppressing people for their faith.

This allows citizens of our nation to dwell together, holding a variety of views on politics and religion. This invites people of conscience to come to a land where they can live their lives according to the dictates of their own heart and worship or not worship as they see fit.

The First Amendment promised us the ability to speak our minds in ways that you couldn't in the rest of the world. To this day, you can say things in the United States that would get you thrown in prison even in "free" countries like Canada and the United Kingdom. The right to a free press that reports information critical of the ruling regime is a gift. In much of the world, those who report the truth do so at the risk of their lives.

Yet this amendment is being torn apart by both sides of the political spectrum. To increase its power, each side seeks to chip away at the nation's most important foundation. To preserve America's domestic tranquility, it's crucial we make good on the American promise of freedom of religion and freedom of conscience.

Discrimination against religion, Christianity in particular, often occurs on campuses. One of the most recent examples was the decision of Wayne State University to decertify Intervarsity Christian fellowship. While all could attend meetings, the group leaders had to be Christians. Wayne State said this violated their discrimination policy when other groups have comparable rules. For example, the college's secularist group requires its leaders to be secularists. Fraternity leaders must be male and sororities leaders must be female. To expect Christians to not require Christian leadership is as equal to expecting the secularists to let a Christian lead them.

Many cultural changes were advanced with the idea of live and let live. In practice, many must cooperate or leave professions and businesses they spent decades building. This is not "live and let live."

In theory, it is possible for society to accommodate both newly invented legal rights and the religious beliefs of dissenters. However, that choice is often not made. Take the case of Kim Davis, the County Clerk who refused to sign Same Sex Marriage licenses. This became a national drama in 2015, with Davis going to jail. It could've been avoided by the Governor of Kentucky taking action sooner so marriage licenses no longer needed signed by the county clerk.

Yes, that's how the controversy was resolved by the new Governor. Same Sex couples in Kentucky can get marriage licenses, and Davis doesn't have to violate her conscience by signing their certificates. Nor do any other couples have certificates signed by the County Clerk, so there's no discriminatory difference between the certificates. Yet the prior governor, Paul Patton (D-KY) chose to instead ignite a needless national controversy.

If it is possible to accommodate a government employee's conscience, it's more so in the private sector. We've seen governments bully religious dissenters in the private sector. These include pharmacists, bakers, florists and photographers. The Supreme Court narrowly overturned the State of Colorado's prosecution of Masterpiece Cake shop owner in part because the State had allowed three other bakers to refuse to make cakes critical of same-sex marriage.

Plenty of businesses are willing to help facilitate a same-sex marriage. The only reason to require anyone to violate their conscience is to squash dissent.

First Amendment rights are also denied in the name of a mother's alleged right to abort her child. Since abortion's legalization, there have been efforts to force medical professionals to perform or facilitate abortions. For instance, some wish to force doctors and nurses to perform abortions in medical school. This would bar the doors to the medical profession to people of several faiths throughout the country.

Freedom of conscience seems dirty in the eyes of a consumer-driven culture. It's viewed as something nasty to cast aside so any consumer can get anything they want from any service provider. We are consumers and we must be served unconditionally.

In June 2018, the conservative group Campus Reform interviewed students on the issue of baking cakes. To a person, they said a baker should have to bake a gay wedding cake. Baking all cakes was his job. If he couldn't in good conscience bake any cake any customer wanted, then he shouldn't be in business. The interviewer asked them if a black baker should be required to bake a cake honoring the KKK, or if a Jewish baker should be required to bake a cake honoring Nazis. The answers changed radically with all but one student.

On some level, we recognize and value the right of freedom of conscience and freedom of religion. However, we tend to only recognize it for people and causes we sympathize with. Yet, for these rights to survive and for our society to be at peace, we have to respect those rights even with people we disagree with and find unsympathetic.

That's where many on the right fall short, particularly regarding Muslims. Many staunch defenders of Christians' religious liberties are aghast at the sight of any accommodation of American Muslims.

Legitimate concerns do exist about the dangers of radical Jihadists. However, this leads to a paranoia and bigotry towards every Muslim. Most Muslims only want to be free to live according to the dictates of their own consciences. Yet Conservatives fear that a school or business making allowances for Islamic dress or diet is moving America one step away from having Shariah law forced upon us all at gunpoint. This is preposterous.

Some even argue that the first Amendment applies only to Christians. A First Amendment that only grants religious liberty to Christians will not have the support of the American public in the Twenty-First Century. That stance thus endangers religious liberty for us all as it will make the public less sympathetic to religious liberty and more willing to tolerate its abridgement.

However, even in the early days of the Constitution, many of America's founders took a far more generous view. Take George Washington's letter to the Hebrew congregation at Newport, Rhode Island:

> The citizens of the United States of America have a right to applaud themselves for having given to mankind examples of an enlarged and liberal policy — a policy worthy of imitation. All possess alike liberty of conscience and immunities of citizenship.
>
> It is now no more that toleration is spoken of as if it were the indulgence of one class of people that another enjoyed the exercise of their inherent natural rights, for, happily, the Government of the United States, which gives to bigotry no sanction, to persecution no assistance, requires only that they who live under its protection should demean themselves as good citizens in giving it on all occasions their effectual support.

This captures the Spirit of America we should aim for. Christians need to support giving other faiths the religious liberty we want for ourselves. That's the only way religious liberty and freedom of conscience can be defended for anyone.

It's important to not treat one religion more favorably than any other. Christians and Muslims deserve equal efforts at religious accommodation. If an airport opens a prayer room at the request of Muslim travelers, it's not unfair for that prayer room to be set up for interfaith use.

Many school districts have gone overboard in trying to teach tolerance for Islam. Some will have kids role play at being Muslims, choose Islamic names, and learn Islamic prayers. This seems to be based on the quaint notion most children come from observant Christian homes and are already fully versed on the major tenets of the Christian faith and history.

In reality, children receive an immersive education on Islam, with generous readings of both the Koran and Islamic history. In contrast, the children's exposure to Christianity is often limited to excerpts from Jonathan Edwards' eighteenth-century sermon "Sinners in the Hands of an Angry God." Parents are within their rights to challenge this biased, unfair treatment of Christianity by the local schools. However, it's not right for such challenges to take on an anti-Islamic tenor. The debate should be about fair and equal treatment in the public square.

Religious liberty and freedom of conscience are challenging issues. But if we lose them, we will lose the core of what makes America a free country.

Freedom of speech is another hot-button issue, particularly on America's college campuses. Public universities often limit the type of speech allowed as well as the places where you can express yourselves.

In addition, a variety of speakers have been disinvited or faced threats of violent protests. There's also the practice of shouting down speakers so no one can hear what they have to say. Some speakers have been worthy of controversy. Milo Yiannopoulos has been a proponent of the racist alt-right movement. Until he was banned from Twitter, he was a leader of anti-Semite trolls, as well as an advocate for pederasty. He's worthy of condemnation, but the violent protests only helped his efforts to stir up animosity.

Campus liberals have shut down all kinds of speakers, including conservative talk show host Ben Shapiro. He didn't vote for Trump. He received a large number of anti-Semitic attacks on Twitter during the 2016 campaign and had to deal with issues on campuses. Even campuses that haven't stopped Shapiro from speaking have responded in unusual ways. Both Berkley and UConn offered counseling for students to cope with someone coming on campus to deliver a speech they disagreed with and were in no way required to attend.

The intolerant PC culture on America's college campuses became a rampant concern. Even Barack Obama condemned it in September 2015 at a town hall in Des Moines, Iowa:

> Sometimes there are folks on college campuses who are liberal, and maybe even agree with me on a bunch of issues, who sometimes aren't listening to the other side, and that's a problem too. I've heard some college campuses where they don't want to have a guest speaker who is too conservative or they don't want to read a book if it has language that is offensive to African-Americans or somehow sends a demeaning signal towards women. I gotta tell you, I don't agree with that either.
>
> I don't agree that you, when you become students at colleges, have to be coddled and protected from different points of view. I think you should be able to—anybody who comes to speak to you and you disagree with, you should have an argument with 'em. But you shouldn't silence

them by saying, "You can't come because I'm too sensitive to hear what you have to say." That's not the way we learn either.

Obama has spoken on the issue several times, including at Rutgers University. In 2014, Condoleezza Rice withdrew as commencement speaker after the faculty and students raised a stink about her invitation. Remember, she was part of the Bush administration and was the first Black Woman to serve as Secretary of State. Obama said, "I don't think it's a secret that I disagree with many of the foreign policies of Dr. Rice and the previous administration. But the notion that this community or the country would be better served by not hearing from a former secretary of state or shutting out what she had to say, I believe that is misguided."

He once again called on students to reason, saying, "If you disagree with somebody, bring them in and ask them tough questions. Hold their feet to the fire, make them defend their positions. If somebody's got a bad or offensive idea, prove it wrong. Engage it, debate it, stand up for what you believe in. Don't be scared to take somebody on. Don't feel like you got to shut your ears because you're too fragile and somebody might offend your sensibilities. Go after them if they're not making any sense. Use your logic and reason and words, and by doing so you'll strengthen your own position. And you'll hone your arguments and maybe you'll learn something and realize maybe you don't know everything. You may have a new understanding, not only of what your opponents believe but of what you believe. Either way, you win."

These are ideals that Americans held for two hundred years. The regime of trying to shut down speech you disagree with has been challenged by none other than Senator Bernie Sanders (I-VT.) He attacked those who got Ann Coulter's speech at Berkley cancelled in April 2017. These leaders on the left deserve respect for standing up for free speech. It shows how far outside of the mainstream the attacks on this American liberty are.

Obama's sensible advice to young Progressives is going unheeded as campus intolerance continues. This should concern Americans whether they are in college or not. These campuses are the training ground for America's future progressive leaders. What is being taught by campus radicals is a course in left-wing fascism that claims a right to shut down speech it disagrees with.

In far fewer numbers, the right has tried to use the same tactics. In a 2017 story, Trump supporters in California shut down a speech by California Attorney General Xavier Becerra. However, such cases remain exceptional.

The main right-wing threats to freedom of speech have been from President Trump. He and members of his administration have called for people in the private sector to be fired. The most notable examples are NFL players who kneeled during the National Anthem. In addition, President Trump called for firing comedienne Samantha Bee for a disgusting attack on his daughter.

Sarah Sanders called for an ESPN radio host to be fired for tweeting that Trump was a white supremacist.

Let's put aside whatever our own feelings are on the targets' controversial and/or plain disgusting behavior. President Trump isn't some guy calling up a talk radio station to express an opinion. He is the chief officer of the Federal Government. On some level, he touches every business in this country. He appoints the Commissioner of the IRS. His statements are chilling threats to punish dissenters with job loss. The NFL introduced a policy of punishing the anthem protests due to the President's statements.

This sets a dangerous precedent. The First Amendment is meant to foster a spirit of how our society relates to one another. It's popular and technically accurate to state private citizens and private companies can't violate our First Amendment rights. However, to keep our freedom of speech and freedom of religion, we do need to respect others' rights to hold their views. We've missed the point when we say, "You have a right to freedom of speech, but I have a right to organize a social media mob to ruin your life."

Celebrities on all sides take a lot of heat from fans who dislike their political opinions. However, most of them will be fine as they have money, status, and power. The true danger of social media mobs comes when the targets are far less powerful.

Take the case of a Utah teenager who posted a picture of her prom dress, a second hand Cheomsam, a traditional Chinese dress. She was cyberbullied by an angry mob for the crime of cultural appropriation. Take the Christian pizzeria owner who answered a hypothetical question on catering a same sex wedding. The shop was almost forced out of business. They received 7,000 negative reviews on Yelp from people who hadn't ever eaten there. They also faced death threats.

Freedom of speech is effectively gone if the people fear a self-righteous mob harassing them and ruining their lives. A society where people can't speak their mind without serious consequences is one where people feel abused and disillusioned. This leads to an openness to violent, extremist voices.

A new political party must celebrate and support the First Amendment rights of all citizens. It should also encourage a spirit of forbearance in dealing with opposing viewpoints.

America's Freedom of the Press is the envy of much of the world. It can be irritating when journalists go after political leaders we like. However, this is far preferable than the situation the rest of the world faces.

At its best, our free press serves as an important check on those in power. People in power on both sides have been willing to undermine that freedom.

Obama's record on the free press was awful. President Obama took office promising transparency. Instead, under him, America sunk from 20th to 41st on Reporter's Without Borders ranking of the World Press Freedom Index.

According to an article in the Hill by Russell Paul Lavelle, RWB was troubled by, "the current administration's obsessive control of information, which manifests itself through the war on whistleblowers and journalists' sources, as well as the lack of government transparency."

CNN's Jake Tapper said, "The Obama Administration has used the Espionage Act to go after whistleblowers who leaked to journalists . . . more than all previous administrations combined."

The New York Times reported in 2013 that the Obama Administration seized two months of phone records from the Associated Press. The Administration gave no notice and provided no reason for the seizure.

In 2015, PBS reported Obama set a record for denying Freedom of Information Act requests. PBS noted, "It also acknowledged in nearly 1 in 3 cases that its initial decisions to withhold or censor records were improper under the law — but only when it was challenged." PBS reported in 2017 that the administration spent $36 million in court defending its decision to deny many Freedom of Information Act requests.

Long before President Trump declared his war on "Fake News," Obama raised his personal war on Fox News. The Obama White House went so far as to describe a News Organization that opposed the President as "not a real news organization."

Obama gets a pass from far too much of the mainstream press because he praises the press. Such as in his last press conference when he said they were, "part of how this grand experiment in self-government works…America needs you and democracy needs you." His fine rhetoric shouldn't give him a pass on actions which undermined the free press.

In addition, due to ideological bias towards Obama, many editorial leaders didn't cover Obama's violation of the rights of the frontline reporters with the same gusto they have with similar violations by a Republican president.

President Trump's war on the free press is rhetorical, but that rhetoric is alarming. Trump has labeled the press as "enemies of the people." Josef Stalin pinned that label on people that his Communist government later murdered.

Barack Obama labeled one organization "not a real news organization." Trump has labeled a host of opposition press outlets as "Fake News." Trump has also stated any negative poll numbers reported were "fake news."

The term "fake news" originally applied to bogus news sites that popped during the 2016 election. Generic sites spread unsubstantiated stories with no byline. Others appeared to be from legitimate news sources. The url contained official-sounding keywords, such as "ABC news." However, discerning readers would note it was a subdomain or a foreign-registered domain name. I noted many friends on Facebook sharing articles from these fictitious news sources.

Some mainstream news sources published lists of these false news sources. They confused the debate by listing valid conservative news sources as fake.

Trump then performed an act of political jujitsu on the media and labeled the opposition press sources as "fake news."

Beyond rhetoric, Trump has carried on the prosecution of leakers and the seizure of phone and email records. So far, his pace has been much slower than President Obama's.

Of greater concern is Trump's war on Amazon. He has pressured postal authorities to raise their rates on Amazon's shipments, which would get passed on to American consumers. Why such animus towards Amazon? Its owner, Jeff Bezos, owns *the Washington Post*. The *Post* is the most anti-Trump mainstream media outlet in the country. Trump means to punish Bezos' digital superstore because he doesn't like what Bezos' newspaper writes about him. If Trump succeeds, this will have a chilling effect on the freedom of the press.

The media is far from blameless. The press has been its own worst enemy with its flagrant bias, lack of responsibility, and a failure to own up to systematic past mistakes coupled with an arrogant self-righteousness. Yet, this is not a reason to give up on the freedom of the press.

Thomas Jefferson said, "were it left to me to decide whether we should have a government without newspapers or newspapers without a government, I should not hesitate a moment to prefer the latter." Jefferson warned, "Our liberty cannot be guarded but by the freedom of the press, nor that be limited without danger of losing it."

Jefferson cherished the freedom of the press while loathing what they printed. A new political party needs to stand firm in support of this essential right, even when we loathe what is written.

On social media, all sides spread too many "alternative facts," as one of the President's advisors called lies. We need unbiased, straight-shooting journalism more than ever. As news consumers, we need to demand it. A new political party needs to stand firm for preserving the freedom that allows the press to be a responsible check on the government. Even when the press isn't living up to that responsibility—and especially when the party deems the press an irritant.

Chapter 16
False Dichotomies

A new must beware of the false dichotomies that hold politics captive. The party always requires the ability to hold important, conflicting principles in a dynamic tension. This ability will be the key to everything else covered in the book, but for now we will focus on party platforms.

For an example of a false dichotomy, while building the platform, the debate may assume we face a choice between being principled or being practical. We need to be both.

If we are practical without being principled, then our platform will say whatever sounds good to voters, activists, and big donors. We'll also do whatever will keep us in power. We'll be a party of immoral liars who worship power. In other words, we'll be the Republicans.

If we are principled, without understanding the concerns and problems of real people or how elections are won, our platform will make pronouncements about the way the world ought to be. We'll sincerely mean it but have no effective plan to enact it and no one will be listening. In other words, we'll be the Constitution Party.

A similar false dichotomy asks us to choose between tolerance and principle. A party can either stand for something or it can be welcoming to people who hold a variety of viewpoints.

Ronald Reagan laid out the case for why principle was important in his 1975 Speech to CPAC. "A political party cannot be all things to all people. It must represent certain fundamental beliefs which must not be compromised to political expediency, or simply to swell its numbers."

Yet, Reagan formed and led a coalition who didn't agree on every issue. A party's platform must lay out core values but still allow room for variation in viewpoints. A successful party will embrace ideas that seem to contradict. For example, practical coalition building and being principled. Rather than choose between them, we must put them in dynamic tension and balance.

This isn't the end of false dichotomies. New political parties will confront many others. For example, some activists will insist a new party must choose between competing in elections for federal office or running strong local candidates, which we will discuss more in Chapter 24.

Political pressure groups like to frame all debates as either/or questions where every citizen will emerge either a winner or a loser. Either you're pro-business or pro-worker. Either you're an open-borders extremist or a xenophobic closed-borders extremist. You either care about victims of campus rape or you care about due process for the accused. You either hate minorities or you don't support the police. You either support job-killing regulations or you hate the environment.

Each of these positions represents ideas that deserve heard respectfully: business, labor, the rule of law, legal immigration, supporting the victims, the rights of the accused, minorities' rights, the police's effectiveness, the environment, and the economy. None of these are things that deserve to be defeated. In fact, to one extent or another, all of these need to win.

For many politicians, putting these ideas in opposition to each other is the key to their success. These false dichotomies drive our politics in the crazy direction, particularly when we respond to craziness on one side by embracing the opposite insanity. A new party must reject the crazy.

Now in saying this, I don't imagine a centrist idea that all of these "sides" need to win that the solution is going to be splitting the difference. The reality of the human condition makes such neat tricks impractical. In some cases, the correct position may be between the two positions, but it may be offering a solution that goes an entirely different direction than both.

For example, there may be a problem where the Republican solution is to create a massive new government agency, and the Democrat solution is to create an even bigger government agency. Ideally, a new political party would offer a solution that didn't require a new program but instead addressed the issue with more respect for citizens and less expense to the country.

The new party's proposals need to be guided by conservative principles, common sense, and a respect for all of America's people and their interests. That doesn't mean we'll make everyone happy;. It doesn't mean we won't be accused of being horrible people who are against minorities, against women, and against clean air because we object to measures that we consider counterproductive. It does mean that, unlike some abusive people on the right, we're not going to do things just to upset people. It means we will be people of good will who honestly and vigorously present our case and work to convince other people of good will to support the party.

Similarly, the party must have a proper view of "compromise." Compromise inspires some to spit in contempt at the very idea. Other, well-meaning voices assure us "compromise is not a dirty word." Which is it? The answer is quite complex.

Some compromises can have horrible results. America is so deep in debt due to compromises by members of Congress. Bi-partisan compromises on budgets often involve an agreement for broad spending increases, driving up the deficit. Alternatively, it means more taxes and more spending now in exchange for promised spending cuts later. This approach to fiscal responsibility is in the spirit of, "I will gladly pay you Tuesday for a hamburger today."

Historians don't look back kindly on past compromises that sacrificed human dignity and human rights for political expediency. In the future, this will go for similar present compromises.

Part of the confusion lies in that the word compromise can mean two different things.

Merriam-Webster defines the noun compromise as:

> 1 a: settlement of differences by arbitration or by consent reached by mutual concessions
> b: something intermediate between or blending qualities of two different things
> 2 a concession to something derogatory or prejudicial //a *compromise* of principles

Per Definition 2, compromise is dirty. If a conservative politician moves halfway to the liberal position without arbitration, this is both a definition 1b compromise and a definition 2 compromise. He's surrendering ground to a side with no interest in negotiating.

Per definition 1a, compromise can be beautiful. The U.S. Constitution is wholly a series of 1a compromises between various fractions in the Constitutional Convention. The delegates from large states wanted a legislature with the seats apportioned by population. The delegates from small states wanted a legislature where the states had equal representation. So we ended up with two legislative houses, one apportioned by population and one apportioned equally.

Compromise happened since the members had a greater cause in common. In the words of the Preamble to the Constitution, they saw a need to, "form a more perfect Union, establish Justice, insure domestic Tranquility, provide for the common defence, promote the general Welfare, and secure the Blessings of Liberty to ourselves and our Posterity."

To do that, they needed a united country. They needed large states like Pennsylvania and Virginia and small ones like Delaware and New Hampshire. They needed to make the Union work for everyone and they came up with a Constitution that did that.

Benjamin Franklin expressed his sentiments on the Constitution well and his willingness to accept it despite some portions he was dubious about:

> "I confess that there are several parts of this constitution which I do not at present approve, but I am not sure I shall never approve them: For having lived long, I have experienced many instances of being obliged by better information, or fuller consideration, to change opinions even on important subjects, which I once thought right, but found to be otherwise. It is therefore that the older I grow, the more apt I am to doubt my own judgment, and to pay more respect to the judgment of others....
>
> "In these sentiments, Sir, I agree to this Constitution with all its faults, if they are such; because I think a general Government necessary for us, and there is no form of Government but what may be a blessing to the people if well administered, and believe farther that this is likely to be well administered for a course of years, and can only end in Despotism, as other forms have done before it, when the people shall become so corrupted as to need despotic Government, being incapable of any other. I doubt too whether any other Convention we can obtain, may be able to make a better Constitution. For when you assemble a number of men to have the advantage of their joint wisdom, you inevitably assemble with those men, all their prejudices, their passions, their errors of opinion, their local interests, and their selfish views. From such an assembly can a perfect production be expected?"

A political party requires compromise. You can't build a broad coalition without it. Yet compromise must be wise and show respect for principle. If you compromise on every issue to build a political party, you will build another vacuous power-hungry party. However, if you compromise on nothing, you'll do nothing more than build another pup tent party that will do little more than massage party members' sense of virtue.

A balanced approach requires defining which hills you are prepared to die on and which you're willing to let go. It also requires respecting what issues are critical to other potential party members. For example, I'd advise fiscal conservatives to consider that social conservatives will never support a party that isn't pro-life. It's prudent for fiscal conservatives indifferent about abortion to accept the party being pro-life so the party can grow enough to get traction on fiscal issues.

Chapter 17
Platform Pitfalls

A new party needs to beware the pitfall of drafting a phantom platform that is celebrated by its authors but ultimately is irrelevant to the real world of politics. An example of such is the 2016 Republican platform. It was the most conservative in history. Donald Trump made no effort to interfere in the platform except to weaken the platform's support for giving aid to Ukraine, a fact that has fueled Russian collusion talks.

However, consider the convention speech of Peter Thiel, PayPal's socially liberal CEO. He slammed the GOP for "distracting fake culture wars" and attacked social conservative efforts to protect businesses from being forced to let transgendered bio-males use women's restrooms. However one feels about that, what was written in the party platform contrasted with what was shouted from the podium at the Republican National Convention.

Trump left the Republican party platform alone because it only matters to the conservative activists and the voted duped into believing it mattered more than Trump's poor character. In reality, the Republican party platform doesn't matter. Trump and House Speaker Paul Ryan released their own agendas that were completely different from the party platform.

If a party platform doesn't tell you what a political party is going to do in power, then what good is it? The platform is irrelevant if party leaders ignore the platform's stated principles and priorities. It's only an attempt to sucker its base into believing the Party stands for something when it doesn't.

A new party has to define its true values and its actual agenda in a platform that is understandable to its members, voters, and opponents.

I had the privilege of voting on a party platform in 2008 as a delegate to the Idaho Republican Party Convention. This was the year that many Ron Paul supporters got elected as delegates to the State Convention and served on the platform committee.

I was surprised the platform called for the elimination of the Federal Reserve and for repealing the Seventeenth Amendment, which changed the Constitution to have Senators directly elected. These were radical changes. I liked the idea of repealing the Seventeenth Amendment, but privately I questioned the wisdom of eliminating the Federal Reserve.

The Federal Reserve has problems with the way it was founded and with its operation, particularly the lack of transparency. However, at the time, the Fed had been part of our country for 95 years. Eliminating it rashly may do more harm than leaving it. I favor auditing the Fed so the public can gain a better grasp of the Fed's operation and management. With this understanding, it could create momentum for reform of our financial system.

However, the platform was a package deal. I could either vote for it all or against it all. In the end, I voted yes, as did most of the Convention.

The floor vote was balanced by other considerations. There was a great desire by the party leadership to resolve all issues on the floor in time for delegates to leave for home. We were expecting (and indeed had) a big fight on the floor over the party chairman race. Any time spent on the platform would detract from that, so the smart thing was to vote yes and be done with it. Like Trump, many Republicans realized the Party platform didn't matter.

Later on, many in the Idaho GOP sought to have Republican candidates for office detail their disagreements with the party platform. By and large, Republican politicians refused. I can understand why Conservatives wanted this. Candidates in the primaries could spout platitudes while never taking a stance on anything, get elected, and govern further to the left than we would prefer.

I can also understand why politicians resisted and why they got away with it. Political candidates are deluged with questionnaires that take hours away from their campaign. The request for information on their views was like this and far longer than most questionnaires. They also knew the platform was read by few Idahoans. It was a document crafted by activists whose main political accomplishment was getting on the platform committee and would never have to defend it to voters. It was passed as written because party rules made it too hard to amend on the Convention floor.

In the end, like most platforms, the Idaho Republican platform pleased the people who wrote it and the activists who read it. However, it fails the test of defining what the members of the Party believe, what the Party's agenda is, and thus what a victory for the Party would mean for citizens of the State.

Chapter 18
Five Rules for Creating an Effective Platform

In the next two chapters, we'll take a look at the big question of how a platform should be written. In this one, we'll offer five general rules of thumb for writing a good platform. In the next chapter, we'll examine what specific planks should be in the Party platform.

1) Don't Overstuff the Platform with Interesting Ideas

Not every interesting idea merits inclusion in the party platform. Take for example repealing the Seventeenth Amendment. When it was passed, the goal of letting the people vote directly was to get the influence of big money and special interests out of elections to the Senate. Today, a direct vote of the people has given more influence to big money and special interests.

In addition, coupled with the Sixteenth Amendment allowing for the Income Tax and the passage of the Federal Reserve Act, America was put on the road to a big spending government that's tens of trillions of dollars in debt.

Prior to the enactment of these two Amendments, if Congress wanted to collect a tax outside of excise and tariffs, it would apportion the tax among the states to collect it as they saw fit. This meant government didn't grow big. One House of Congress was accountable to state legislatures. If Congress apportioned a high tax, it was up to the State legislatures to collect it. This ensured Congress didn't pass some big-ticket item that would require the States to raise massive amounts of money. If Congress did that, it would be politically fatal to the Senators who went along with the effort.

With the Sixteenth Amendment, Congress obtained unlimited access to tax the people's income. With the Seventeenth Amendment, the Senate was no longer beholden to state legislatures. The Federal Reserve would make it easier, in time, for the country to finance greater and greater amounts of debt. Those three changes from the early part of the twentieth century are the seeds of the massive, intrusive federal government and the out-of-control national debt we have today. The federal government expanded and began to take on more and more powers that the Constitution had reserved for the states.

The states have made some pretense of fighting for their constitutional prerogatives. However, the states and local governments spend an unseemly amount of time trying to beg for money from the Federal government to fund their pet projects.

Repealing the Seventeenth Amendment would be a step back to restoring the balance the Founders intended. The people would still influence the senate race, as candidates for the state legislatures would campaign as the Senate candidates' de facto electors. Currently, voters have more influence over who sits in the State Legislature than they do in via multi-million dollar Senate campaigns. If we kept big money and special interests out of the state legislature races, the people's franchise would take minimal damage or even be improved.

However, as good an idea this is in theory, it doesn't belong in a party platform. Consider the aftermath of the Idaho GOP including it in their platform. The media had much fun with the new platform planks. The plank regarding the Fed was not controversial among average voters. The state's general population lacks trust and understanding in the Fed.

However, voters were puzzled why the Republican Party wanted to take away their right to elect their U.S. Senator. Meanwhile, many politicians were eager to curry favor with the activists who inserted the plank and embraced it. However, they didn't understand the reasoning behind it, which lead to some cringe worthy moments during debates as they struggled to explain why they supported changing the Constitution.

To this day, the media use this as a gotcha question. If targeted Republicans support the platform, they risk alienating voters and coming off as cranks. If they oppose repealing the Seventeenth Amendment, they risk alienating the party regulars. Thus the GOP has handed journalistic hacks an easy tool to derail any conversation about the party's serious agenda.

A party platform isn't for "good" ideas. It is for the party's *core* ideas: the legislative platform that the party will pursue and the key values its members hold. Good ideas should be advocated for, but not in the party platform. Advocates for good ideas need to explain and spread their ideas until they reach a level of public support that makes them plausible, feasible, and helpful ideas.

2) Keep the Platform Simple

God gave us all minds to reason with. Yet some activists strive to make the party platform cover every situation. The goal seems to be for our elected officials to mindlessly follow the platform without question, embracing it as their guide for every single issue.

The result has been massive platforms that politicians don't respect and most voters haven't read, including advocates for following the platform. The National GOP platform is fifty pages long, and the State parties all have their own platforms. In Idaho, the platform is fourteen additional pages long. All this detail isn't controlling politicians' behavior. It's wasting paper.

A national or state party platform should be no more than three-to-five pages long. That's plenty of space to provide a general preamble of the party's values and beliefs and spell out the party's program for the critical issues facing the nation or the state. Further, it would be prudent to release for voters an easy-to-read synopsis of the full platform no longer than 350 words.

A concise platform will make it easier to hold elected officials accountable. When a platform is overstuffed with nonessential or obscure planks, it's easy for politicians to ignore the platform.

If your platform consists of only ten-to-fifteen crucial planks, it's easy to measure whether a political leader is supporting the party's ideals.

Even with a more focused platform, unanimity on every point doesn't need to be required. Reagan once observed, "The person who agrees with you 80 percent of the time is a friend and an ally—not a 20 percent traitor."

As a general rule, if a candidate agrees with the party on twelve out of fifteen planks, they should have no problem within the party. However, if a candidate only agreed with nine planks, I would look elsewhere for a candidate for office. A party needs to be broad enough to have room to attract many leaders and build a successful coalition while still holding to core principles.

3) Remember You Can't Start the World Over Again

Thomas Paine wrote in *Common Sense,* "We have it in our power to begin the world over again."

This idea resonated with Americans in the Revolutionary War era and in the era of Ronald Reagan. Yet, the truth is, in politics, we can't entirely escape the impact of past generations' decisions or the environment we begin with. The Revolutionaries and Reagan made big changes but they were hampered by the institutions that existed before them.

If conservatives started an independent colony on Mars, we'd do many things differently than on Earth. We wouldn't set up a retirement system like Social Security. Home schooling and private schools would be normative. Any public instruction would be based upon the majority religion, with accommodations for non-adherents. Numerous government functions on Earth would wisely never get introduced on our own little independent colony.

Barring going to another planet, we can't begin anew. We must recognize where we're starting from. It's a country where we've had progressive income taxes and the Federal Reserve for more than 100 years, big government programs from the New Deal for over eighty years, and the Great Society welfare programs for half a century. These programs have changed our culture.

The business of a new party is to begin from the world as it is, and to propose changes that will move the country we have in a better direction.

4) Include Long Term Goals

In addition to immediate legislative priorities, the platform will contain long-term goals. The balance will be between immediate and long-term goals.

Having recognized where the country is, a new party will define where it wants to take the country in the long-term. Some priorities might be, "Reduce the size and scope of the Federal Government," "Balance the Federal budget," "Ensure legal protection for human life from conception until natural death."

Long-term goals are just that. When the party gets into power, these goals will not all be achieved in the first 100 days. Our system of checks and balances makes quick changes hard to achieve legitimately. Problems generations in the making will be generations in the solving.

A long-term policy goal will be viewed like a goal in football. The party's leadership will be expected to move the ball forward towards the goal. If they succeed in that, then reasonable members will be happy, but everyone needs to keep their eyes on the long-term goals to avoid complacency.

5) Avoid a Self-Centered platform

The Libertarian Party focuses upon legalizing all drugs. The Constitution Party focuses upon disentangling the U.S. from the rest of the world. Focusing on the issue they care about is their right, but it's part of the reason why these parties have failed to win major elections.

To win an election, a party has to speak to the concerns of voters, which are most often not the party ideologues' concerns. The big issues for voters are things like the economy, health care, immigration, and the general disorder and corruption in the government. At the state level, education is also a big issue. A party that fails to address these issues will not succeed electorally.

A party doesn't need to adopt the Democrats' big government philosophy. We can't beat the Democrats at finding ways to make government bigger and more intrusive (though the Republicans have certainly been trying.)

The voters' concerns need to be addressed with solutions that lead to less dependency, less government, more freedom, and more opportunity.

The Libertarian and Constitution Parties are proof America isn't looking for a new party that only cares about their pet issues. People want a new party that cares about the issues that concern them. If all they see is people riding political hobby horses, they'll have little interest in giving that party their votes.

This benefits the causes closest to conservatives' hearts. I'm strongly pro-life and I believe it's important to elect pro-lifer leaders. However, it's vital that pro-life leaders be ethical, competent, and address the issues that concern the whole electorate. If they take care of the people's prime concerns, they will be electorally successful and be able to do more for the pro-life cause.

The greatest defeats for conservatives has not come from voters rejecting conservatism but from rejecting the leaders who fail to competently, ethically address the issues on American's minds. A new party will learn the lessons of the past and make intelligent decisions for a better future.

Chapter 19
Planks a Platform Should Include

Many books have laid out a step-by-step platform for a party or political movement. Other books present the same material as a noted authority's political prescriptions for everything.

That is not my goal. Any political party worth its salt is not going to get its platform from a book. Its members will brainstorm ideas to address the problems of the nation. A united group of people of good will would come up with better solutions than I ever could alone.

However, I will suggest three planks I believe a platform should include.

Platform Plank 1: Government Reform and Integrity

Both parties are full of opportunistic, unethical, and dishonest people who have fostered great cynicism in American politics. Both have shown a willingness to be indecent and unkind. Both have engaged in race-baiting and identity politics. An effective new party will take a new direction. It will be clear from the outset that it will stand for clean and ethical government.

Some of this will be in the party's preamble. This will contain a statement of general principles and core philosophy. However, specific actions will also be called for. It's important to avoid a cynical populist claptrap which offers grandiose, unrealistic reform measures.

Take, for example, Lamar Alexander. In his 1996 Presidential campaign, he rose to the top tier of GOP contenders on advocacy for limiting Senators to two terms and taking radical action against congress. His slogan was, "cut their pay in half and send them home." By "send them home," he meant to make Congress part time.

In 2002, Alexander was elected to the Senate. He made no effort to cut Congress's pay or to limit Senators to two terms. He is now Tennessee's senior senator and serving his third term.

Making Congress part-time is unworkable with government at its current size. With its current schedule, the size of the federal government has meant that Congress struggles to get its appropriations bills passed and get votes on key executive branch appointments as a full-time body. Even if you believe the main purpose of Congress is repealing unnecessary laws, there are so many of those, a part-time congress would never do. Like much of Alexander's campaign, it sounded good, it looked good, but it was ultimately empty.

Term limits is a challenging issue. Politicians who favor term limits often refuse to term-limit themselves, arguing that places their party at an unfair disadvantage. They'll vote for term limits but until it becomes the law of the land they will serve as long as they can get re-elected.

I understand term-limit advocates' reluctance to "unilaterally disarm" by imposing term limits on themselves while their opponents re-elect members of Congress forever. However, it's past time for such arguments. Americans have been lied to by far too many politicians and have grown tired of parties who talk about reforms they won't live by. It's not enough for a party to talk the talk about clean government. They must walk the walk.

Any platform plank on government reform needs to be enforced by the party apparatus. The issue of term limits is a great example. One key argument for term limits is "power corrupts." Washington, DC has a morally corrosive atmosphere. Those who stay too long get drawn into its culture, come to view Washington as the best venue for solving the nation's problems, and develop an inflated view of their accomplishments and abilities. Career politicians believe they are indispensable to good government. Others become so corrupted by flattering bureaucrats and lobbyists, they believe they're above the rules and unaccountable.

The premise of term limits is, the longer a politician is in Washington, the more likely they are to succumb to its toxic culture. Why then would a party consider it an advantage to prolong a member's Congress service? This only makes it more likely that they will lose touch with their constituents or become ethically unhinged.

If a new party commits to term limits as part of its platform, it should enforce that on its officials. If the Party decides in its platform that a member of the U.S. House should serve no more than four consecutive terms, it should be a party policy that when a member of the House runs for a fifth term, every officer of the Party must oppose the incumbents' re-nomination.

A party that favors term limits will also impose them on the party's internal leadership. Leading a party is different than holding an elected office, but there's a tendency in political organizations to become too much a part of the system. In addition, the party can become more successful by introducing new blood and new ideas. A party or organization led by the same people for years has trouble adapting to new challenges.

It is important term limits be reasonable and well-thought out. A group labeling itself the Federalist Party of America (not the actual Federalist Party) launched and declared there would be a one-year term limit on its leadership positions. This is a problem. Elections happen over a two-year cycle. A one-year term limit keeps a party from having consistent leadership within the same election cycle. It's important to balance the need for fresh ideas and new blood with giving a leader space to lead and forge a direction. Changing the leadership every year will leave a party spinning its wheels.

A policy I recommend would be to limit leadership posts to four years, as either two terms of two years or one term of four years, depending on how the party is organized.

In some states, candidates for the state legislature aren't required to provide financial disclosures. If these states' parties decide that this should change, they should require it of their own candidates.

If a new party wants to show the public they are different from the corrupt, existing party, it must form a firm principle of not saying, "Elect us and we will pass laws to ensure the right thing is done," but instead, "We will do the right thing as a matter of policy and principle."

Finally, government reform proposals should be reasonable and workable. It is important to avoid demagoguery which leads to over-the-top promises that cannot be kept. This temptation must even be avoided when talking about Congress.

It's easy to take potshots at Congress and suggest, if we treat them harshly, we can solve all manner of ills. Congress's perennial low approval rating ranges from the high single digits to the low teens. If you want Americans to applaud, declare we can fix America's problems by putting all 535 members of Congress in a darkened room with a single candle and feeding them only stale bread and lukewarm water until they solve everything.

This is nonsense that fails to understand how Congress works. Members of Congress set their own pay, benefits, and working conditions. They would never vote for my example, nor would they vote to eliminate their health care benefits or to eliminate their pensions or to cut their pay in half.

Second, it misidentifies the motives of members of Congress. It is popular to pretend that a high salary and great benefits draw members of Congress.

The truth is many, if not most members of Congress, could make more money in the private sector. Time Magazine reported in 2014 that, for the first time ever, a majority of Congress were millionaires.

Wealthy people run for Congress for many reasons. Some do want to add fame and power to their wealth. A few are there to serve their country. Anyone motivated by money views Congress as a step toward their post-Congressional career, where they'll earn big money as a lobbyist, or working at a think tank, or serving as executives the companies they regulated. No one is in Congress for the pay and benefits package.

Such talk is rabble-rousing that smart voters will tune out. To stand out, be honest with the American people about the needed changes and avoid the demagogic nonsense.

At the same time, an effective new party will avoid meaningless gestures that hamper party growth. For example, the Federalist Party of America said they would not be accepting donations of more than $100 due to the corrupting nature of big donations.

This gesture may be sincere. However, cynical Americans who understand politics will view it as virtue-signaling. Kinder experts will view it as clueless naivety. Millionaires are not inclined to plunk down tens of thousands of dollars to corrupt a startup political party without any ballot access. The Federalist Party of America is pledging not to accept donations that were not going to come in the first place.

More importantly, it may tie the hands of future leaders and make getting the party off the ground nearly impossible. If the Federalist Party of America does get to the point of forming state parties and a real national organization, the national leadership will be hampered by this term-limit. If they change it in light of circumstances that arise when financing a real political movement, they will be branded as hypocrites. If they keep the limit, they will not be able to be a competitive political party.

It is principled to avoid the appearance of corruption and strive to be a party of the people. Perhaps a certain dollar amount of donations does by its very size corrupt the political process. Even if you do believe that, it's hard to argue that the corrupting number is $100.01.

If a new party is to make a financially self-limiting gesture, it should make a realistic one. If a startup party refuses to accept donations nobody was going to send, no one cares. Let's take a party that has gotten into double digits in statewide races and won a few elections. That party could decide to not accept donations from Corporations, Corporate PACs, or individuals of more than $5,000. That would convey it is serious about remaining free from corruption.

A National Party making that decision will also understand its impact and will be able to make that decision without crippling itself.

Platform Plank 2: Federalism

Federal elections are treated with far more serious focus than in past years. Much is at stake. Issues from abortion to religious liberty and same sex marriage all come down to how the moderate justice on the Supreme Court votes. At the same time, Washington is flush with cash and regulatory power. Who runs Washington can make billions of dollars of difference for businesses. The decisions made in Washington impact nearly every aspect of our lives.

Who runs the Federal Government has become too big of a deal. This was not how the Founders intended it. James Madison wrote in the Federalist Papers (#45), "The powers delegated by the proposed Constitution to the federal government are few and defined. Those which are to remain in the State governments are numerous and indefinite. The former will be exercised principally on external objects, as war, peace, negotiation, and foreign commerce; with which last the power of taxation will, for the most part, be connected."

If you want to calm the national political angst, end the reality that major decisions are being made in the most corrupt city in America. Move power back to the states and to the people.

Unelected judges misusing their office to make law undermines respect for the rule of the law. Our voice as voters can be overridden by judges who want to write law rather than interpret it. This is poisonous. It makes the appointment of Supreme Court Justices far too important.

One solution is found in the text of the Constitution. In Article III, it lays out in what specific cases the Federal Courts are guaranteed jurisdiction. It includes this note, "In all the other Cases before mentioned, the Supreme Court shall have appellate Jurisdiction, both as to Law and Fact, with such Exceptions, and under such Regulations as the Congress shall make."

Congress can limit the jurisdiction of the Supreme Court and other federal courts. Many Republicans fear the consequences of limiting the jurisdiction of the courts on controversial issues. While those concerns are real, the consequences of not doing anything are serious. A toxic national culture war consumes politics because of a Supreme Court that can't stop itself from inventing new rights that were never in the Constitution.

Next let's consider federal spending and regulatory power. There are three ways to deal with excesses in these areas. First, eliminate federal agencies that intrude on matters best left to the states. This is ideal but hard to do. These agencies have patrons in Congress and a media that confuses eliminating an intrusive a federal agency with opposing the ends of that agency. It's possible to be for education but think Washington, DC should have no role in it. Getting rid of the Department of Education and similar unconstitutional agencies is a heavy lift.

Another possibility is to rewrite the agency's missions and scopes. For example, most states have agencies tasked with protecting the environment. Why should the federal EPA interfere in an issue that can be addressed effectively by state agencies? It'd be better to limit the EPA's action to addressing issues with interstate consequences.

Finally, we could cut federal bureaucracy by sending money to states in block grants. For example, the Federal Department of Education runs numerous school programs. Block grants would replace these. Funds would be designated for specific purposes such as Pre-K, elementary education, or special education but would let the states develop their own programs.

A state bureaucrat is not naturally more virtuous or capable than a federal bureaucrat, but she does have some advantages. She's closer to the people and is more likely to understand their specific needs than someone in Washington, DC. She's also more likely to interact with the programs created and experience the consequences of the regulations.

Most importantly, state agencies are more accountable to voters. If a local school district is failing us, we can get involved and vote the school board out. If our state education department introduces a flawed policy, we can lobby our state legislators, who are usually more accessible than members of Congress. The Superintendent of Public Instruction is usually subject to a vote of the people and thus can be removed. However, if a bad federal education mandate comes down, we can do little besides complain.

If we increase the number of government actions that people can impact, and decrease those that are made for them in Washington, DC, we'll have better government, and we will also reduce the feeling of powerlessness that makes our national politics so toxic.

Platform Plank 3: The National Debt and Entitlements

According to the US debt clock, on 6/19/2019, the national debt was approaching $22.4 trillion dollars. At its current growth rates, on 6/19/2023, the national debt will be approaching $29.7 trillion. The most important measurement is the nation's debt to GDP ratio. That was at 105.5% on 6/19/2019 and it will pass 121% in 2023 if our current growth rates remain stable. This shows our nation is seriously over-leveraged.

Most people agree the national debt is a problem in theory. However, the popular fixes involve raising taxes on "the rich" or cutting waste from domestic spending. We imagine our debt and continued deficits are caused by $600 toilet seats being bought by the Pentagon.

Our annual deficit is more than a trillion dollars. Government should cut out waste, fraud, and abuse. Taxpayer money should not be spent frivolously. However, we're kidding ourselves if we think our national debt is caused solely by $1 million for an idiotic research study or $250,000 for a museum promoting an obscure cause in the middle of nowhere.

To get serious about our debt, we have to get serious about entitlements. Our federal budget is $4 trillion. More than $2.1 trillion of that is Social Security, Medicare, and Medicaid spending. Another $300 billion is spent on SSI, Unemployment, and food stamps. We are paying $300 billion per year in interest on the national debt, and that is only going to rise.

The left resists any changes to Social Security or to Medicare, as do older Americans who typically lean conservative. I'll address mostly the arguments raised by older conservatives.

The challenges to changes to Social Security fall into two categories. First, are questions about how the system has been run by Congress. Some claim that Congress stole money from Social Security by putting Social Security surpluses into the general fund. This myth is so often repeated, the Social Security Administration addresses it on its website:

> There has never been any change in the way the Social Security program is financed or the way that Social Security payroll taxes are used by the federal government. The Social Security Trust Fund was created in 1939 as part of the Amendments enacted in that year. From its inception, the Trust Fund has always worked the same way. The Social Security Trust Fund has never been "put into the general fund of the government."
>
> Most likely this question comes from a confusion between the financing of the Social Security program and the way the Social Security Trust Fund is treated in federal budget accounting. Starting in 1969 (due to action by the Johnson Administration in 1968) the transactions to the Trust Fund were included in what is known as the "unified budget." This means that every function of the federal government is included in a single budget. This is sometimes described by saying that the Social Security Trust Funds are "on-budget." This budget treatment of the Social Security Trust Fund continued until 1990 when the Trust Funds were again taken "off-budget." This means only that they are shown as a separate account in the federal budget. But whether the Trust Funds are "on-budget" or "off-budget" is primarily a question of accounting practices-- it has no effect on the actual operations of the Trust Fund itself.

The truth is that Lyndon B. Johnson wanted to achieve a balanced budget without having to cut spending, so he used an accounting trick to make the budget look balanced. Johnson and the Democratic Congress were guilty of lying, not of massive theft of Social Security funds. Even if Congress had spent the funds, what could we do about it now?

The problems with Social Security is it was created for a different society. People had far more children then and died at younger ages. Back when Social Security was passed, the average life expectancy was less than the retirement age of 65. Increases in life expectancy coupled with lower birth rates means less workers to support an ever-increasing number of retirees.

According to the Mercatus Center at George Mason University, in 1945, there were forty-five workers for every retiree. In 1960, that ratio sank to five to one. Now, there are only three workers for every retiree.

Another distracting argument imagines that Congress's pension plan gives members of Congress their current salary for the rest of their lives. This myth further states, if we took their pensions away, they would solve the problem of Social Security. A mutant variant of the myth states the average congressional pension check is so much greater than the average Social Security check that the only Social Security fix needed is eliminating congressional pensions.

This is all nonsense. The congressional pension is a normal pension based upon the years worked and the age at which the recipient retired. The longer a member of Congress serves, the more they earn. According to the Annenberg Center for Public Policy, this cannot exceed eighty percent of their final salary. To get that high of a percentage, a member of Congress has to serve for a very long time. For example, Senator Tom Harkin retired after forty years in Congress and he received seventy-one percent of his final salary.

The idea members of Congress are concerned about their pensions assumes that members of Congress are there for the benefits. Members of Congress don't address Social Security because they would like to be re-elected.

Now, the average Congressional Pension is indeed more generous than the average Social Security check. However, there are more than forty-five million Social Security old age and survivors' recipients, and a little more than six hundred Congressional pensioners. If you could take away every congressional pension, it still would not make a dent in the entitlement crisis.

The most compelling argument is fairness. Retired workers have good reason to chafe at being lumped in with other entitlement recipients. Often, they worked their whole adult lives, and each paycheck had hefty deductions for Social Security and Medicare. They supported past retirees on the promise they would receive the same benefits when they retired. Cutting their benefits violates this promise. This is a fair point, which makes alternations to Social Security and Medicare different than changing Medicaid or Food Stamps. The latter programs are paid for from general revenues based on government generosity.

Yet a fairness question exists for today's workers, too. We didn't create the Social Security and Medicare crisis, yet we are all paying for it, even as our own retirement prospects dim. Consider the price the boomers' grandchildren and great-grandchildren will pay for this unsustainable system and the danger its collapse will pose to their economic health.

According to the Heritage Foundation, by 2037, the cost of the Federal Government as a percent of the GDP will reach 40%, driven by higher spending on Social Security and Medicare. Further, 10-12% of GDP goes to State and local taxes. We are looking at a situation where more than half of our nation's annual wealth will be government spending, stifling economic growth. At the same time, the Social Security Administration stated, by 2035, the Trust Fund will be exhausted and annual revenues will only be enough to pay 75% of retirees' earned benefits. The seniors on Social Security will face a massive benefit cut if nothing is done.

Both parties have failed on this. Democrats like Daniel Patrick Moynihan and John Breaux saw a need to reform the system but have long since departed the political stage. The current crop of Democrats want to "scare the seniors" away from any effort to make entitlements sustainable. Republicans had made tentative efforts at reform but had no communications strategy and controlled both houses of Congress, knew a crisis is coming but were too cowardly or to selfish do anything.

A December 5, 2018 report in *The Daily Beast* stated, when presented with data showing the coming spike in the national debt caused by his irresponsible spending and failure to make needed reforms, President Trump said, "Yeah, but I won't be here." Many politicians over the decades have similarly chosen to "kick the can" down the road for someone else to deal with so they can get re-elected.

A new political party will shoot straight with the American people. Making changes to the system is not fair to the seniors. However, it is also not fair to the seniors' young grandkids and great-grandbabies to leave an unsustainable system to collapse and bring economic ruin on them. It's selfish for any adult to refuse to make hard changes necessary to protect today's kids.

This mess has been created by demagogues and powerful lobbies that sing a siren's song to keep Americans blind to the true state of affairs. A new party should provide an honest and thoughtful wake up call.

It will require a long-term strategy. It will leverage less expensive medical technologies like telemed to reduce costs of routine doctor visits. It will introduce work requirements for able-bodied adults in non-retirement entitlements and find ways to wean these adults off government dependence.

We will consider encouraging people to look at alternate views of retirement. In the 1930s, Congress envisioned a broken-down miner retiring at age sixty-five to spend his last three or four years of his life resting, with his widow surviving him by a couple of years at most. This isn't the case today. Retirees are far healthier and active than they were in prior generations.

What if, at age sixty-five, a worker could take a one-year sabbatical and receive benefits, provided they forestalled retiring for five years? This could be offered every five years, allowing them to recharge in exchange for delaying full benefits further. This would allow them to enjoy a productive career that will allow them to save more for when they permanently retire.

Many older workers are not tired of working but of doing the same kind of work. What if older workers could take up to two years off to train for new careers and pay for it with a tax-free withdrawal from their IRAs or 401(k)s? Rather than consider retiring early from careers wearing them out physically and/or mentally, they could begin new careers that are less taxing on them and could keep working until their eighties.

The problem is complex and multi-layered. The solutions will have to be equally complex. The new party will need to come up with changes that will not only ensure current recipients of Social Security and Medicare are cared for, but that America becomes sustainable and remains a land of opportunity for generations to come.

Chapter 20
Advice for Would Be National Party Leaders

I have witnessed several failed Presidential campaigns and failed third-party efforts. Their own bad practices ultimately doomed their efforts. My advice is to do the opposite. This is no guarantee for success, but failure to follow these basic steps can doom any effort before it gets started.

Gather Your Team

No one in their right minds plans a major undertaking without first considering what it's going to require of us and making preparations. Yet numerous campaigns and parties have not had these conversations and they have not gotten advice from any people who can help them succeed. Before you start the party, you need to have enough people to support a professional operation.

The ideal is for part of finding the team to involve finding the fundraisers and the donors. Here, we're not looking for millionaires but for enough people to give funds to get started. It's important to have the right people in place to have a party that presents itself professionally.

While Americans hate professional politicians, they do require professionalism from their political parties. The party's website should look modern, not like something that belongs in the Internet Archive from the 1990s. Emails should be answered promptly. Anyone who answers the telephone should use proper telephone etiquette. Do the little things and do them well.

Don't rush to anoint state coordinators

I've written about independent candidates or third parties and received offers to help organize my state on their behalf. When I was young and naïve, I was flattered. As I've grown older and wiser, I now see it as the ultimate sign a political organization is an amateur hour. The ability to write a column and the ability to organize a state are two different talent sets. The offer suggests a bit of desperation as well as a lack of professionalism.

The political amateur starting an organization is driven to have states organized ASAP. The sooner we appoint state coordinators, the sooner we can put out a press release boasting of how many states we're in.

The problem is, I've been in campaigns that boasted of over forty state coordinators but missed the ballot in most states. Those coordinators existed solely on paper. They were encouraged to take the title but they had no time or talent to do the job.

Pushing people to become state coordinators risks turning off the volunteers who find that position's commitment too overwhelming. A 20-something state coordinator who can't handle that responsibility could have instead been an eager petition-carrier or envelope-stuffer.

Before you appoint a state party coordinator, first find out who the person is. In the Twenty-First Century, there's no excuse for not Googling someone. On one campaign, I discovered a key state leader had a record of advocating for murdering abortionists. Thankfully, I discovered this before the media did, informed the campaign, and the campaign dealt with it.

Talk to your prospective state coordinators. Ask about their employment history, what their values are, and what their experience is in politics. Are they a leader? Do they know how to respect people different from themselves or do they live to create drama? It is better to not have a state coordinator than to have a toxic person who breeds bad feelings. The national coordinators don't need to waste campaign resources on cleaning up after bad state coordinators.

Also ask about the prospective state coordinator's availability. Someone who organizes a state party needs to travel across the state. This is more challenging in large states like California or Montana than geographically small states like New Hampshire and Rhode Island. In large states, consider appointing regional coordinators, so no one has to carry a huge travel burden. It's also key to be self-employed or to work for an employer that offers great flexibility.

Choose wisely in appointing a state coordinator, or your national organization will suffer. In the 2000 presidential primary, I collected most of the required signatures to get a candidate on the Montana ballot, sitting outside stores in the bitter cold of winter. I was asked to serve State Coordinator for the campaign. I tirelessly lobbied state legislators to endorse the candidate and got a good handful of endorsements.

In late May, the candidate's new national grassroots coordinator arrived to meet with me and he was not pleased by my efforts. Looking back, he had many good points. I hadn't done lots of things a state coordinator needs to do. However, the person who had appointed me had failed to note I was then a nineteen-year-old with no savings and a job in fast food. I had neither the flexibility or the resources to travel the state of Montana, nor did I have a rolodex of contacts. I also wasn't provided direction on what I should do, so I made things up as I went along.

If you appoint a nineteen-year-old fast food worker with no resources to run your state operations, then you get the results you deserve. That goes for appointing any state coordinator whose main qualification is not being savvy enough to know they're unqualified.

The appointment of state or regional coordinators will not always be necessary. A party needs to get signatures to get ballot access. However, this most often can be done with someone who doesn't wear a title but explains the ballot access requirements to local and county groups and gets them information.

In my home state of Idaho, we need 13,848 signatures to qualify a new party. A wise petition gathering effort will aim for 27,700 signatures due to issues with unqualified signatures. The majority of that could be gathered in Ada County and the neighboring Canyon County. In a state like Idaho, it makes sense to start with a petition-gathering effort launched by a state-level Facebook group. Once the party makes the ballot, then have the local party hold a state convention and elect their own state leaders.

Other states makes this formulation less feasible. They will require many signatures from every county or Congressional district. This may require more active hands on management. If that's the case, then find someone appropriate. Don't just grab the first person to contact you via the Internet and toss him or her into the deep end. Doing so will hurt your efforts and cost you whatever this person could have done effectively for the party.

Remember Activism Needs Activity to Thrive

If there's anything more disheartening than amateurish organizations desperate for help, it's when you express your interest in a party or candidate and never hear back.

Often times, it's due to poor planning. The person who set up the organization didn't make sure he or she had enough people to handle the email.

When someone visits a website for an unfamiliar political organization, a nerve has been touched. There's a flicker of interest in the politics and movement you're proposing. Sometimes organizers imagine if they have gotten someone's attention, that person will be on-call and ready to go whenever they give the word. This isn't always the case.

With some people, if you get back to them within six hours, the flicker of interest will have already gone out. However, for other people, the difference between a prompt response and a response a week later is the difference between a flicker becoming a flame or it going out.

When you get back to them, you need to have a call to action ready. It's not enough to just acknowledge them and say they'll be contacted by a County Coordinator once one is appointed. That might as well be pouring a bucket of sand on the flicker. If you want them to get involved, engage them at once. If you're ready to begin a petition drive or have a local organization that's supporting a candidate, the answer should be simple. However, if not, you'll need to come up with some other ways to keep them engaged.

Some things to consider asking them to do are:

1.	Host a House Party

House Parties allow interested voters to invite friends and family who may be interested in a new party. Generally, a DVD about the party will be played, although a party organizer might be able to make an appearance via web conferencing software. However, the latter option can easily become a comedy of errors that distracts from the new party's message rather than attracting.

A new party doesn't need to produce a House Party packet before it launches its recruitment efforts. However, a packet needs to be in the works. It should include a professional video, literature that can be handed out, and a sign up card with lots of options for getting involved. The host may be asked to pay a small fee for the packet, which is reasonable when the party is getting started.

2.	Write Letters to the Editor

It may seem old-fashioned, but some people still read newspapers, or at least their online editions, including the online editions of the letters to the editor. A letter to your local paper will not be read by as many people as it would have been twenty years ago, but it will be read by more people than a comment in the middle of a threaded conversation on Facebook.

3.	Conduct Research

A new party has a vital need for knowledge of local voter preferences, politics, and legal systems. Also request research on the local election laws, local culture, and local economy. A successful party will ask many questions on these topics and get detailed answers. Doing this research isn't for everyone, but it would keep quite a few activists engaged in a truly productive manner.

4.   Join a Meet Up or Social Media

Local Meet Up groups would discuss party developments, how projects are progressing, and how to do outreach to potential new activists. For a free option, create state-level Facebook groups where members can interact, share information, and coordinate their efforts. Note care must be taken to avoid these action groups degenerating into heated political discussion groups.

Note these are only basic ideas of how to get people started volunteering. A top priority should be developing additional activism outlets. This could include traditional party activism, such as collecting signatures, supporting candidates, and dropping literature. Once the party begins having candidates run for office, it will consider setting up an online phone bank, so party members from areas that lack local candidates can support other areas' candidates.

Whatever the case, your top job is to engage your volunteers and to keep them engaged.

If you want to build a great party, it can't be "your party."

When organizing a political party, it's important to understand your role. Do lay out general principles you and other organizers want the party to represent and set out to attract people who share those valued. However don't attempt to be the be-all and end-all of party policies and the master of all strategy that the party will use.

When you begin to state, "This is our party strategy" or lay out detailed plans on the issues, you're not building a party for conservatives or federalists. You're building a party that promotes you and your vision and implying that everyone else exists to serve that.

A successful party has to be "our party." It has to be open to people coming in with their own ideas to contribute. If you truly are the most brilliant strategist and political thinker ever seen, prove that in an open exchange of ideas. Making a great play about your amazing strategy or long-range goals can present barriers to membership.

A party organizer needs to understand their role is interim if it is legitimate. You can start a website and list yourself as "National Party Chairman." However, you're just a person who has started a website until you've organized the party, gotten it onto state ballots, and held a national convention where the delegates have elected you to lead the party. The initial party organizers' job is to get the party to a point where it's on state ballots and can legitimately elect national leadership. Likewise, the state and/or regional coordinators have no real authority until they are confirmed by the local parties via a legitimate electoral process.

Elected party leaders still need to show humility and not throw themselves into every fight, while being willing to listen to alternate viewpoints. One of their functions is to make peace with the factions found in any vibrant political party. Wise party leaders maintain credibility with as much of the party as they can. Good leadership will do their best to listen to and to empower all party members, not dictate to them from on high.

Chapter 21
State and Local Leaders:
Know Your Stuff, Know Your People

Most people have never been part of the leadership of a statewide party. The good news is these functions can be learned if you take the efforts to learn to do it right. Numerous books, seminars, video series, etc. detail how to run for political office and how to run political organizations successfully. It's safe to say most third-party leaders don't bother with such. They're more likely to be reading an Ayn Rand novel or a political philosophy book. They show no sign of having studied what practical steps to take to get people elected so they can turn their philosophy into public policy.

Leaders who wish to be effective will study the art of politics. The nature of a new party's beginning could mean a leader has to quickly form an organization and figure things out as he goes in a mad dash to the election. However, if a leader is going to continue any length of time, he would do well to find out what is the right thing to do.

Many books cover topics such as how to run a campaign for local office, as do various political field manuals. The online trade publication *Campaigns and Elections Magazine* has many useful tips and insight into the worlds of campaigns and campaign strategy.

Effective leaders won't limit their learning to resources targeted towards conservative independent campaigns but will also consider tools and resources designed by both Republicans and Democrats. For example, liberal former House Speaker Tip O'Neill wrote *All Politics is Local,* a great book on politics and how to relate to people. It's out-of-print but is easily purchased through Amazon or requested through interlibrary loan through your public library.

The Leadership Institute is a conservative leadership training program started by long-time Republican National Committeeman Morton Blackwell. The program is non-partisan and can help people become better party leaders and better candidates.

Other books lay out general campaign principles or provide inside looks at successful campaigns. Campaign documentaries can also help you to identify best and worst practices.

In choosing resources to use for your development as a party leader or as a candidate, it's best to read books suited for your level of campaign. If you are a county chairman in a rural county, a book about Mitt Romney's 2012 campaign will not help much with your own position.

Some books can be read solely for insight into how the opposition works. *Rules for Radicals* by Saul Alinsky lays out the behavior that many on the left use to bend society to their will. Many Trump supporters have also implemented these practices, particularly ridicule. In the book, Alinsky takes time to praise Lucifer. The result of the book's advice has been Satanic as well, slowly eating away at our national civic culture and deepening our divide. A good party will not take advice from *Rules for Radicals*.

Consider reading books on how politicians spin the media. Howard Kurtz wrote a good one on the Clinton Administration's methods in *Spin Cycle,* where he explains how they played the media to distract from the scandal and ensure Clinton's re-election. The book is not to be a guide for a new party on how to manipulate the media. What Clinton did was sleazy and the media is far less likely to cooperate with a conservative third party.

Amanda Carpenter's *Gaslighting America* is a vital book exposing the evil, abusive nature of Trump's psychological manipulation to destroy his opposition and control the country. It is an important book to read to understand what the President does and how to not let it get to you. What it's not for is learning about Trump's evil tactics in order to implement them ourselves.

Similarly, take an article on how the Republicans and Democrats use the multi-million-dollar voter data programs they already have. This is not going to help a new party to recreate that while short on resources. Rather that article, along with *Spin Cycle,* and *Rules for Radicals* can give a party leader insight into how his opponents think.

This demystifies the major parties. Oftentimes, minor parties issue declarations that make defeating the two major parties seem impossible. Sometimes, the major party's power is mythologized by crediting their success to international conspiracies and backroom secret manipulations. A third party's efforts are futile if the two major parties are winning due to secret black magic.

An effective third party is able to say, "These specific things are how the major parties beat us. What can we do to overcome these disadvantages?" This gives them an actual chance to win. Their head is in the game and they're looking at the real situation as opposed to making the parties so mythically powerful there's nothing to be done.

Effective local leaders will also get to know volunteers before they get involved at a serious level in the party. It's not customary for a party to do full background checks on their volunteers. However, if you end up electing Miss Ku Klux Klan of 2010 as your Vice-Chairman and you could have avoided that with a Google search, it'll be a costly and unnecessary mistake.

Beyond avoiding embarrassment, it's important the party network with volunteers and learn about them. What's their past political experience? What's their occupation? How much free time do they have? What are their values? These are the type of things you need to know.

Sometimes, political candidates and campaigns need people to get basic jobs done: stuff envelopes, make phone calls, and drop literature. However, some people could provide more help to the party if you know who they are and what they can do.

For example, imagine a party has six volunteers who are former call center supervisors and two volunteers who are copywriters. The party doesn't know this. So, when it sets up a phone bank, it asks someone to supervise it with no call center experience and has someone write the call script with no experience at writing copy.

This is an absurd situation but it happens all the time. Parties develop an inner circle of folks who get appointed to handle assignments while volunteers are assigned only basic tasks. A new party should be smarter and look for the best person for the job.

It's important to be sensitive to volunteers and accept the help they want to give. Someone skilled in an area does not necessarily want to volunteer in that area. Some retired call center supervisors may never want to hear another ringing telephone as long as they live. The college professor who spends thirty hours a week lecturing her students may not want to spend her free time doing public speaking for the party. However, it's foolish to assume this is the case.

Party leaders will face a number of obstacles and will lack of number of resources. They shouldn't suffer because they don't understand the resources they have in their own people.

Chapter 22
Establishing the State Party

Establishing the party at the state level will involve gathering signatures to get either the party or a specific candidate on the ballot. This chapter is written for State Party affiliates of a new national political party. However, citizens of a state need not be part of a national movement to form their own political party. Dozens of political parties only exist on a single state's ballot.

As long as they're able to meet your state's requirements, groups of citizens can organize a party within their state which can run candidates for local and state office, congress, or governor. If your state has fair enough laws and enough citizens to pull it off, then by all means, go for it. Build your state party and focus on your state.

A single-state party may be able to get involved in the Presidential race. For example, the Independence Parties of South Carolina and Minnesota gave their ballot line to Independent Candidate Evan McMullin. In addition, single-state parties can affiliate with national parties that support their values. For example, several single-state third parties became affiliates of the Constitution Party in the mid-to-late 1990s. If you do start a new conservative party in your state and, two years later, you find an effective national conservative party, you can affiliate with that party and be ahead of the game by one election cycle.

When you begin the process of starting a new party, you need to learn about the process and requirements of getting a candidate on the ballot.

First, how do you qualify? In most states, a petition can pre-qualify your party to nominate candidates to be on the November ballot. In other states, you can collect signatures to get the candidate of the party on the ballot. If that candidate gets a certain percentage of the vote, then your party can be qualified for the next election without the petition drive.

Second, you'll need to know the number of signatures needed, the time frames for collecting the signatures, and where the signatures can be collected. Some states only require you gather a certain number of signatures. Others require these signatures come from multiple Congressional districts or counties.

Also be prepared with contingency plans. Find out how many signatures are required to qualify an Independent candidate for various offices. If one of the focuses of your party is on supporting a presidential candidate, it may be easier, at least in this initial election, to get the candidate on the ballot rather than to qualify the entire party.

Third, you need to find out who may collect signatures and what the law is for signature-gatherers. For example, can supporters of your new party who live outside of your state come collect signatures? Does the person collecting the signatures need to be a resident of the state? Do they need to live in the county they're collecting signatures in? These are all questions that need to be answered. Many a petition has been disqualified because the signatures weren't gathered in accordance with state laws.

Ballotpedia.com is a great resource with an overview of all of these requirements. However, it's best to check with your clerk and recorder's office for the exact information.

With this information gathered, the party leadership will have to make a choice. Depending on the logistics, the number of candidates the party already has run, it may make sense to pursue full ballot access for the party or it may make sense to run a series of Independent campaigns. If half a dozen people want to run only for county commissioner and state representative, focusing your efforts on a simple ballot access process for those individual offices could allow you more time, energy, and resources to win.

If you're in a state that allows initiatives, it may be worthwhile to draft a state initiative to change ballot access regulations. Many conservatives are wary of the initiative process with good reason. Our form of government is a republic where we elect leaders to pass laws. The biggest problem with the initiative process is it produces so many different initiatives that voters have to make a quick decision on with little knowledge. Emotional appeals from self-serving interest groups lead to the passage of legislation a well-informed, accountable legislature would reject.

However, the initiative process is appropriate for the regulation of ballot access and elections. Ballot access regulations are designed to put hurdles in front of the candidates running outside of the two-party system without establishment support. These laws are passed and protected by the well-established legislators representing the major parties and you can hardly expect the legislator to change them to make them fair so others can compete with them.

One key reform would be to reduce the signature requirements for candidates and parties to obtain ballot access or to allow petitioners to pay a filing fee in lieu of gathering signatures.

The sole legitimate reason to limit ballot access is to ensure the ballot is not cluttered with cranks. A reasonable filing fee of $1,000 for statewide office and smaller fees for congressional and state legislative races can stop cranks as effectively as a petition while also saving the state government money.

This would allow the party to not spend so much time just to get our candidates on the ballot. That is only fair as major party candidates don't have to go to this effort. It would save taxpayers money because under the current system, government employees spend countless hours verifying signatures, and if they do disqualify enough signatures, then there's an internal appeals process and perhaps an appeal through the courts. All of this costs money. It would be easier if the only thing the County Clerk or Secretary of State had to ask before listing a candidate on the ballot is, "Did the check clear?"

Voters are fair minded on ballot access and are far more open to reform than state legislatures. Still, initiatives are a challenging task and a new political party is unlikely to accomplish this on their own. It would be appropriate to reach out to all other third parties in the state, including the Libertarians, the Greens, the Constitution Party. The existing minor parties have been able to cooperate on issues of mutual interest. Combining forces would increase the chances of success in the petition drive and in getting it passed in the general election. A successful ballot issue would give party members a taste of victory and encourage their continued involvement.

Third parties can pursue other ballot initiatives together also. Maine recently approved ranked choice voting. This system allows the people to vote third-party without feeling they're throwing away their votes. Under an instant runoff system, voters mark whoever they want to as their first preference and then mark other choices on the ballot in order of preference.

So they could vote for the new party's candidate as their first preference in a three-person race. If that candidate finishes third and neither the Republican or Democrat have won a majority of the vote, then those who voted for the third-party candidate's votes get transferred to their second preference. Of course, if the new party's candidate finishes first or second, then the votes of the third place winner could either make them more successful or cost them the election.

Some advocates of third parties believe in a fusion system where a candidate can carry the nomination of multiple political parties. This can give minor parties influence over the political process because major party candidates may come to them for their support. It also means, on occasion, members of the minor party can get the major party's ballot line. This happened a few times in New York State as members of the Conservative and Liberal parties have at times secured the nominations of the Republicans and Democrats.

However, the idea of fusion should be entertained with caution. For the Conservative Party of New York, fusion has not been a net positive. The focus of that Party isn't on nominating its own candidates but on rubber-stamping the GOP candidates. They mainly have forced the GOP to avoid nominating a candidate too liberal to win the Conservative Party endorsement. You can be pretty liberal and still win it. George Pataki, the most liberal, pro-abortion candidate in the 2016 Republican presidential field, was endorsed for Governor of New York by the Conservative Party of New York for Governor three times.

Any endorsement of a candidate of another party should be limited to cases where the party has no candidate in the race and the individual endorsed truly represents the values the party believes in.[2] On the other hand, it could be a benefit by allowing the party's nominees to seek the endorsement of another party. Each state party should make their own decision on this issue.

However, it's important a party does not focus all its attentions on laws relating to elections and ballot access. If the party does decide to work to pass initiatives, it shouldn't do this to the detriment of promoting its own message and candidates. The party should exist to advance an agenda the people care about, not just to ensure its own existence.

If you live in a state without an initiative process, tuck proposed changes to your state's electoral system into your party platform's government reform plank. Major party leaders will not make anything easier for Independent candidates or new parties. Voters won't care enough about it to impact their votes. Focus on doing the right things at the local level and delivering a positive message that resonates with voters. Your party may have an opportunity to make changes to the state electoral system once you win elections.

---

[2] Cross-endorsing another party's nominee when you haven't nominated a candidate doesn't require having a fusion system. Unless state law prohibits it, a party can pass a resolution to endorse the candidate at its convention.

Chapter 23
The Challenge of Local Politics

Imagine if Gary Johnson had won the 2016 presidential race. How much of the Libertarian agenda would he have implemented?

Even in a Libertarian wave year, they would not muster enough Congressional candidates to take over Congress. President Johnson could only change America to the extent that the Republicans and Democrats allowed it. That is unless he used executive orders to bend the country to his will. Libertarians could work hard to win the Presidency and gain nothing.

Americans view the Presidency as all-important and the state government is viewed as more important than local governments. In my home state, Idaho, people only voted in the May primary when the Presidential nomination had been on the ballot. Never mind that the nomination was a foregone conclusion by May and the Presidential primary was pointless on the Republican side. The state, county, and congressional primaries are far more important than a Presidential nomination that's already decided. However, your average voter doesn't see it that way.

Our Founding Fathers created a nation where we have three branches of government: legislative, executive, and judicial, and all three are coequal. And recall Mr. Madison's words from Federalist #45, "The powers delegated by the proposed Constitution to the federal government are few and defined. Those which are to remain in the State governments are numerous and indefinite."

In many instances, we've gotten away from the wisdom of the Founding Fathers. A federal behemoth has taken a greater role in our lives and the states and localities relate to it in a way they never would have dreamed. Many local governments spend a lot of time figuring out how to jump through the right hoops to get a little bit more federal cash.

I understand why the people are so concerned about the president. The POTUS has always been our national representative, our head of state, the face of the America to the world. In the wake of World War II and the Cold War, the president has become the most powerful man on Earth and the leader of the free world.

The president's power has increased through using Executive Orders to usurp the legislative branch's powers. President Obama declared, "I've got a pen and I've got a phone!" He used that to legalize many illegal aliens when Congress wouldn't act. Most political experts agree the states can't nullify federal law. Yet Obama decided to stop enforcing federal law against marijuana in states that have sought to nullify it. He didn't like the federal law on marijuana and allowed states to nullify federal law because he felt like it.

The judicial branch's encroachments on to the legislative and executive powers have made the Presidency a focus since he appoints federal judges, including the Supreme Court. Our rights are no longer seen as irrevocable gifts from God that the Constitution secured. Instead, our rights are the Supreme Court's property to give and to take away. On a whim, the Supreme Court can restrict our freedoms to the point of effectively revoking them. Every Presidential election, people vote like their entire way of life depends on who wins.

The administrative state has grown to point where the Executive office is becoming ever more imperial. This is only partly why few conservatives are involved in local politics.

Modern conservatives' motives differ from liberals' motives in general. For many on the left, such as the government employees' unions, government largesse is how they live. For others, government is a way of forcing everyone to fall in line behind their vision for society. It also provides personal fulfillment to enact a new regulation or government program.

Conservatives usually aren't inclined to use the government to meet such needs. We often become involved in politics because we have been "messed with." That is, a conservative often first gets involved in local politics after getting an eye-popping tax bill or having a close encounter with an overbearing bureaucrat.

Due to this, liberals can hold sway over local government even in a conservative district as long as they don't get too cocky and don't pull a culture war stunt that lands their city council or school board on Fox News. Even if they do create an outrage, they may weather the storm if they do it far enough out from an election.

In Boise, the city leadership created a great controversy when it decided to remove a Ten Commandments Monument from a city park in January 2004. Outraged residents pledged to fight the city and to remember the officials who ignored the concerns of citizens. By the time of the November 2006 elections, the issue had faded into obscurity. Most of those who initially showed up had disappeared despite their promises of active vigilance in city government.

Another challenge is that many tired of liberal governance opt to vote with their feet. I've observed this on the state level, with Californians moving to Idaho. I've also observed this locally, with many of Boise's conservatives moving to more conservative and less costly cities like Meridian and Nampa. In contrast, liberals as a general rule tend to dig in and seek to force their community to change to suit their preferences.

Another difficulty is the people don't easily understand local government bodies' exact function. Much of what a county commission, a city council, or school board does is not newsworthy. There are tedious conversations about aquifers, personnel decisions, and minor zoning disputes. Unless a controversy erupts, most citizens remain in the dark about their local government.

When most citizens don't know what their government is doing, few will feel compelled to run. I've seen conservatives run for local office with no clear idea of what they would do if elected. One candidate for County Commissioner gave a presentation for his candidacy where he did nothing but read quotes from Ronald Reagan off his cell phone. Others only make vague promises like lower taxes and reduced government spending.

On occasion, such a vague campaign may win. Most of the time, the winner doesn't do well. In some cases, once in office, they outrage their base by supporting more taxes or increased spending, leading to accusations of lying. Most likely, the candidate didn't lie, they didn't know what they were talking about. Once in office, they found pressing needs like a school building which desperately needs replaced and realized they didn't understand the situation. If they had understood it in the first place, they may have been able to put forward an alternate proposal.

How to approach local races and engage people is a tricky question. The proposed Federalist Party focuses on local races. Its founder JD Rucker writes on its website:

> Our focus on local, city, county, and state elections at this early stage in our development is strategic. It's a waste of time, talent, and treasure to throw out sacrificial "protest" candidates to run in races we have no chance of winning. This doesn't stop other third parties who love to throw their resources towards big national races in hopes of drawing attention even when they know they can't win. We view it differently…We need Federalists in place as state legislators, mayors, and even governors.

There will come a time when we're ready to win U.S. Senate seats or even the White House, but we're not going to bypass the low hanging fruit and waste the resources given to us by those who believe in our cause.

Rucker has some points. Local races are important. Parties should avoid simply running warm bodies as token candidates. The exception is if maintaining ballot access requires a certain number of candidates filing, as is the case in my home state of Idaho.

Also, a constant state of losing is bad for the morale of a political party. Rucker proposes to prevent this by avoiding high-profile races the party would be likely to lose. However, in doing so, he leaves his new party with no candidates in races that voters and activists care about most.

What drives interest in a new party is disenchantment in the two parties and alarm at what the federal government is doing. Rucker's plan fails to address these voters' concerns. A political strategy is likely doomed if it ignores voters' concerns. At minimum, its success depends upon getting voters to care about what the party thinks they should care about.

Not all losing is equal. It's disheartening to lose presidential election after presidential election with the major-party rejects and people who couldn't win a county commissioner race anywhere. However, sometimes out of a losing campaign can come the seeds of victory.

For example, George McGovern's far-left 1972 Presidential campaign lost forty-nine states and he lost the popular vote by more than twenty points. Yet that campaign launched the start of many political careers. For example, McGovern's Texas state coordinator was nearly elected to Congress in 1974, was elected his state's Attorney General in 1976, and eventually became the 42nd President of the United States, none other than Bill Clinton.

Similarly, many conservative activists of an older generation traced their involvement back to Barry Goldwater's spectacular landslide loss in the 1964 presidential election.

Pat Robertson's failed 1988 Presidential campaign spawned the Christian Coalition, which was a major power in Republican politics for over a decade.

If you have a losing candidate who connects with people, inspires them, and gets them involved, that can plant the seeds of future activism.

Imagine a businesswoman coming to the Federalist Party in her state to talk about a run for the U.S. Senate. She has a great life story, she gives a good speech, connects great with people, and is with the party on its core values. She doesn't have a fortune to invest, but she is willing to spend tens of thousands of dollars of her own funds and knows people who could raise more. Following Mr. Rucker's sage advice, the Federalist Chairman would have to say, "I'm sorry we don't run Senate candidates. How about running for City Council?"

This would be a waste. A new party should embrace a candidate like this. She can draw crowds and volunteers and that means opportunity. A campaign isn't just an opportunity to win an office, it's an opportunity to engage voters and to identify talented, quality people who could make good leaders in the years to come.

A major campaign offers a smart party a chance to get people passionate and engaged in the process for decades, if it handles the race well. A strong showing can set the party up for success down the road. Third-party advocates point to Abraham Lincoln's success in 1860 presidential election. It would never have happened had John C. Fremont not finished a strong second in 1856 and established the Republicans as the Democrats' chief challengers.

However, local government offices are not "low-hanging fruit." From a national party perspective, that's true. Were a Federalist Party member to file for the local city council, all the national party would have to do is put a link to the candidate on their webpage and maybe put out a press release.

For the candidate, it's only easy to run a bad campaign. Pay a small filing fee, slap together a Wordpress site with a few political clichés, don't bother to research the local needs, fill out the questionnaires from Conservative pressure groups, ignore the liberal ones, and maybe attend a public forum or two. You spend less time on your whole campaign than your average college football fan spends watching the game on Saturday. You won't win that way.

Running a good campaign is hard. My home city's government is officially non-partisan, but the entire City Council is made up of liberal Democrats. Generally, some conservative offers opposition. They pay their filing fees, raise a few thousand dollars and run an active campaign during the six weeks prior to the election. I've asked myself, what would a conservative need to do in order to do better? Here's a list of items I came up with:

1) Attend several City Council meetings to get a feel for how the city government works and the type of issues addressed.

2) Attend meetings of all neighborhood associations in the City of Boise, listen to people's concerns, meet people, introduce yourself. In the city of Boise, there are more than thirty such associations, so be prepared for a lot of nights at meetings.

3) Review newspaper articles on city issues, recently passed city ordinances, and city contracts.

4) Prepare a complete platform of ideas to improve the city in accordance with Conservative principles.

5) Formulate a plan to get the conservative South Boise out to vote to balance out the liberal North End, which controls city elections by turning out while the rest of the city stays home.

6) Raise tens of thousands of dollars to run a city-wide campaign, print yard signs, mail out absentee ballot forms.

7) Campaign door-to-door through the city beginning after Labor Day.

Executing this plan would take a year to complete, a thousand hours, and tens of thousands of dollars. Even then, the candidate might still lose due to the liberal advantage in the city. The council races are held in the odd-year elections with low conservative voter turnouts.

Admittedly, Boise is an extreme example and may not be representative of the local races termed "low-hanging fruit." It's a fair-sized city which elects every member of the City Council at large rather than by using a ward system. This forces City Council candidates to campaign to the whole city rather than just a portion of it.

However, I'd argue similar hard work is required for every local office in the country. As a party-building strategy, running for local office is dubious. As of March of 2018, there are 158 Libertarians holding elective office, as do 25 members of the Constitution Party. Among them are a Dakota County (Minnesota) Soil and Water District Supervisor, and members of the Grand Rapids Community College Board of Directors, a member of the Van Nuys (CA) Neighborhood Council, and the Ken-Caryl Water and Sanitation Board in Colorado.

The good news is third-party candidates can win these types of elections. The bad news is that picking "low hanging fruit" failed to make these parties grow and failed to achieve their goals.

I don't suggest a party wait for the perfect senate candidate to waltz in to inspire its base. It will run candidates for local offices. However, don't force a choice between running a credible campaign for federal offices people care about and running vibrant campaigns for local office. Running on all levels at once is important if we want to be more than just a minor concept party.

Chapter 24
The Importance of the Local Party

You can't overestimate the importance of vibrant, strong, local party organizations. If you lack a sufficient number of them, you can put out press releases, run social media campaigns, and offer good candidates, but it will all be for naught. In this chapter we'll examine the foundation of the local party, its functions, and its best practices.

Foundation of the Local Party

The precinct is the most basic political unit. People in the same precinct vote at the same polling station and live in the same neighborhoods. It should be the long-term goal of any political party to have at least a precinct captain for every precinct.

What you call the precinct captain and how many you have may be governed by state law once your party is recognized and on the ballot. For example, in Idaho, the position of Precinct Committeeman is open to both genders and elected in the May Primary for all political parties. In Montana when I ran, every precinct had a committeeman and a committeewoman.

If your party is not on the ballot or if your state has no law, the titles and structure will be up to the local organization. If a State has a law, a wise local party will follow it even if they aren't officially recognized yet, so they can transition to official status as quickly as possible.

If party organization will always be up to the party, then consider the option of having a Committeeman and Committeewoman from each precinct or have an A and B position for each precinct. The more people who are active and involved in the party, the better. Another way to increase membership is for each Precinct Captain to have an alternate to represent their precinct and ensure a quorum at county party meetings.

Electing precinct captains can happen in two ways. If your party is recognized and your state holds elections for precinct officers for third parties, then elect the leaders at the primary elections. Otherwise, elect your leaders at a precinct caucus. For most Americans the word "caucus" conjures the Iowa presidential caucus. However, the caucus is used by parties throughout the country for party organizational purposes.

A good practice for a new party would be to lay the groundwork for the precinct caucuses by seeking out people to open their homes for house parties. Hold informational meetings about the party's ideals and goals and arrange the details of the precinct caucuses in as many precincts as you have people interested in the new party.

The precinct caucus may meet at local homes but could meet in a conference room at a public building like an elementary school. For simplicity's sake, multiple precincts may hold meetings at the same venue if it has enough rooms available.

How the caucuses and the precinct meetings are conducted will vary in accordance with state laws and any decisions made by the national party. I won't go into all of the possible combinations and potential procedures. However, whatever process is followed must be orderly. Meetings must be conducted in accordance with basic rules. Roberts Rules of Order remain a simple operating procedure that nearly any assembly can adapt.

Both State and County parties should have written by-laws that are accessible to read. The State Party should set requirements for county parties but be flexible. For example, take the election of officers. Having a Chairman, Vice-Chairman, Secretary, and Treasurer is the ideal arrangement. However, some counties with large populations may have two vice-chairmen who are charged with different tasks. Smaller counties may have to combine some of the roles such as having a Vice-Chairman/Secretary.

Organizers of a County Party convention will have someone working on draft rules. Various models of party rules can be a basis for a governance model with adaptations. The rules will be subject to amendment and adoption at the organizing County meeting.

For many activists wanting to make the world a better place, getting procedural ducks in a row is tedious, boring stuff. Yet, it is vital. Well-written and thought-out rules provide a framework for orderly conduct of party business and serve as a safeguard against abuse.

Psychologically, it provides weight to the proceedings. Doubtless the party will begin over coffees and informal dinners. It's a long journey from there to an organized party. The passage of rules signifies this is a real party now and it sets the tone for orderly proceedings.

One final caution on organization. Your party may borrow structural ideas from local major party groups. Be cautious about overextending yourself by trying to match their functions.

For example, the major party may have precinct captains in ninety different precincts. You may only have twenty captains in the same county. If you try to have all the same functions and offices as the major party has, you're going to end up having unqualified people filling them.

Functions of the County Central Committee

What does a Central Committee do? Many traditional roles are often neglected by minor parties. First, is working the precincts. Precinct Captains do things like walk their precinct, handing out literature in support of the party's candidates. Ideally, you will recruit volunteers to help you. With enough helpers, you can do a task like that in a few hours.

Some prefer the approach of knocking on doors. This can be intimidating and leads to some mixed responses. If you're skilled at it, it can also connect with people who wouldn't consider voting otherwise.

A second function of the central committee is raising money. This is vital and most minor parties remain massively underfunded. There are numerous ways to fundraise. Direct solicitation is obvious, but four-digit and five-digit donors are not likely to be common. A wise new party will find creative ways to raise funds. Pie auctions, raffles, and contests with entry fees should be considered as well as events.

The major parties have a practice that minor parties should emulate. The Republicans hold Lincoln or Lincoln/Reagan Dinners. The Democrats traditionally hold Jefferson/Jackson Dinners. Democrats in many states have shifted to Kennedy/Clinton Dinners due to Jefferson and Jackson having owned slaves. Regardless of what they're called, these dinners serve three purposes: fundraising, socializing, and education.

A new party could hold a similar dinner, with another historic figure as the symbol. A Washington Day Dinner held around Washington's Birthday could be a great idea. The basic formulation would be to set reasonable ticket prices that pay for a nice dinner, a good speaker, and turn a profit. The key to success in the immediate and long-term is to make this an event that people will truly enjoy. If the guests have a good time, then the dinner can also be used as a recruitment tool.

A great asset to the party would be someone who can come up with creative and fun ways to raise money. As always, be sure to research your state laws on fundraising and political parties.

A third function of the central committee is recruitment and outreach. Committee members should be on the lookout for individuals of compatible beliefs and appropriate temperament to run for office and fill vacant committee seats. Much of this will occur in casual circumstances.

In addition, a party should be out in the community with informational booths at public events. Places like county or regional fairs where businesses and other political parties have booths are potential places to introduce the Party to a broad group of voters.

The party can consider venues that Republicans would not attend due to the existing bias against the GOP. However, it must be careful not to over-extend itself. Instead, focus on events that will provide an opportunity to reach a high number of voters receptive to its message.

In addition, in a functional state, the local party will elect delegates to the state convention. Many minor parties don't practice that to their detriment.

Once someone tried to recruit me into a minor party to get rid of a troublesome state leader. I was informed I could switch party affiliation right after the Republican primary to the minor party. I could drive to the minor party's state convention and just by being registered with the minor party, I could be a delegate, capable of voting on party platforms and setting the party's rules. I could even switch back to Republican after the Convention.

A new party would be wise to avoid inviting such mischief into their state organizations by having delegates elected by the local party.

Local parties can also pass resolutions on any topic. This can be overused. A local Central Committee's major task is to build the party organization and support the party's candidates. In addition, many resolutions are ill-conceived and ignore how the media will portray them. They are non-binding except regarding party governance. A poorly thought out resolution serves only to stir up unnecessary controversy and to detract from the party's mission. As such, I recommend resolutions be limited to party business. For example, a resolution calling for an action to occur at the State Convention, such as the passage of a platform plank.

These are the core functions of the local party. If you re-examine the challenges to a City Council run, you will note an effective local party backing the candidate would help greatly.

A local party needs people who will research state and local politics and educate potential candidates. This could take the form of in-person training or a written manual. This will detail basic facts such as the functions and scope of government agencies, salary, and job requirements of local offices. It will also provide an understanding for the key issues facing each office.

The researchers would provide the candidates the data they will need to run an informed campaign. This campaign may still need to do some research on its own, but it would at least give the candidate a leg up. It's ideal to have multiple researchers, so you get multiple perspectives.

You may also have researchers who produce a manual or training for the candidates interested in running for the legislature. However, this is something the state party may also commission.

While You're Waiting For the Revolution....

What if you're in a state where you lack ballot access? Maybe few counties have active interest in the new party, so you don't have the potential of a true state organization?

You can still do some of the functions above. If you find a good candidate for partisan office, you need to get creative to get your candidate on the ballot.

It may make sense to run them as an Independent. It may be an option for a candidate to run under another party's ballot line. The Libertarian and Constitution Party have ballot access yet they don't run any candidates in countless races. Only pursue such an alliance if the other party's local leadership is easy to work with and if the local party's image is not problematic.

In addition to the known national minor parties, many state parties may be compatible with your party or may be non-ideological (such as many Independent/Independence Parties.)

As a non-recognized party, also consider endorsing candidates of other parties. Avoid a "lesser of two evils" endorsement. Instead, endorse a major or minor party ticket that represents the type of ticket your party will nominate. If the party endorses the candidates, encourage the party's members to volunteer within the candidate's organization.

This serves two purposes. First, it provides an outlet for activism to help elect a candidate who will do well for the people of his state. Second, it allows you to observe a campaign in action. This will allow you to pick up best practices and note unproductive behaviors.

In addition, our own state parties and our own candidates for high office would set up virtual phone banks with call from home programs. This would allow people in states without organized parties or candidates to help the party's other candidates. The party's success in one state could create more interest in the party across the country and improve its ballot access.

A local party could run a book club. Some books would focus on practical application of conservative principles, others would focus on the art of politics, and others would focus on general topics like persuasion that have a political application.

Most critically, the local party leadership's primary job is to "keep the band together." This means providing meaningful activities that allow members to impact the political process. This also means providing educational and social opportunities that will keep people plugged in.

Chapter 25
Advice for the Uncommon American Citizen

Many Americans are concerned about where our country is going and understand the state of our current political affairs can't go on forever. However, many don't have the time or interest in becoming a party precinct leader or going to monthly political meetings. If you're one of those Americans, what can you do?

First, avoid political parties and projects that aren't worth any investment of time, energy, and resources. In this book, I've laid out the actions a serious political party should take. If you see a new party emerge, then evaluate if their efforts are serious, if they have the attitudes of people who will succeed, and if they are making decisions that will set the party up for success. If the answer is no, then avoid investing your time, money, and energy in the new party.

Unserious efforts end up being harmful. They invariably ensnare people who are sincere but inexperienced, get them excited, and then disillusion them and burn them out.

If you've been involved in a minor party or political group that proved to be dysfunctional, then prepare yourself mentally to try again. However, this time ensure any efforts are on the behalf of an organization that knows what it's doing and thus is functional and well-organized.

Second, provide the party occasional help. Political parties need two types of volunteers: full-time regulars and people who help out once and a while for the big things. The second type of volunteer generally gives a few hours every now and again.

Short-term activities may include:
- Holding a house party.
- Collecting signatures to get a new party on the ballot.

- Attending precinct caucuses.
- Election-day related volunteering.

The house party and the caucuses require a set amount of involvement. Most other activities will depend on your own personal bandwidth. You could take an entire day to go outside a large venue and collection 900 signatures, or you might grab a petition and get a dozen friends to sign as you happen to see them over the course of a month.

You could dedicate two hours a day for weeks leading up to the election. You could volunteer on election day by working the phones or serving as a poll watcher at your polling place. You could spend a half-hour twice a week making "get out the vote" calls from home.

A related way to support a new party is through financial donations. Few of us can underwrite a Super PAC or write a big check for the federal maximum of $2800 to a political candidate. However, we can give a little, maybe $5, $10, or $20 per pay period.

This may seem paltry. It is fair to ask what $5 is supposed to accomplish or if collecting twelve signatures from your friends is going to make a big difference in a state where tens of thousands of signatures may be required to get a candidate on the ballot.

We hear about new records being set for the most expensive campaign ever all the time. The numbers are overwhelming. They make what we can do seem insignificant and irrelevant. No wonder many Americans have embraced as their political messiah a billionaire with a strongman persona who pledged that "I alone can fix it."

Remember two things when looking at the goliath budgets of big political figures. First, this is overkill. Many campaigns raise big money and still lose. At the national level, consider the fundraising prowess of Mitt Romney's 2008 Presidential Campaign or Jeb Bush's 2016 effort.

Consider Jon Ossof. According to the New York Times, Ossof raised $23 million for losing a special congressional election in Georgia. Campaign consultants will never admit it, but there is such a thing as enough money. Spending beyond that is of limited usefulness. In fact, if all that money buys ads that turn off voters, it may be counter-productive.

Second, small individual efforts matter when large numbers of us do our bit. There are many historic examples of this. One is World War II, when the entire nation came together in the war effort. America's success came through the bravery of our Armed Forces and also the determination of people on the home front. They made personal sacrifices. You had millions of people doing little things such as taking part in scrap drives or growing their own food in Victory Gardens. The nation had war bond drives, with the kids taking part by spending their dimes on "war stamps" which could be redeemed for bonds. All these little efforts allowed America to fight and supply our forces overseas.

Today, we live in a world of crowdfunding: GoFundMe, Kickstarter, Indiego, Patreon, and Subscribe Star have changed the way we do business. Some businesses and products exist solely because enough people kicked in $5, $10, or $20 for an idea that they believed in. Films and television programs have been made on the same basis.

The little we have to offer can make a difference. Take 500,000 people (less than 1/6 of 1% of our country's population) and imagine them volunteering four hours total in a year. Imagine them giving a small contribution to the new party and its candidates out of each bi-weekly paycheck of between five and twenty dollars, with an average gift of nine dollars. Those 500,000 people would provide two million volunteer hours and contribute $117 million. That's significant, not small. It's the type of serious effort that will inspire those who care about our country and have more resources to expend them.

At the end of the day, we all have to do our best and to hope others care enough to do their bit too. Together, we can accomplish great things.

Another small difference you can make is to educate yourself and your sphere of influence to become better news consumers. If we're going to engage with the politics of our country, then we have to know what's going on in this reality.

Sadly, many conservative news sources have transformed into click bait and state media propaganda. They succeed by keeping their readers in a constant state of fear and outrage. The main exception as of this printing is National Review, which in 2019 still published a variety of conservative news and opinion. The columnists that hadn't yet caved to Trump were David French, Jonah Goldberg, and Jay Nordlinger of National Review, Susan Wright of the Resurgent and Patheos.com, Ross Douthat of the New York Times, and Matt Lewis of the Daily Beast.

The mainstream media has its own agenda and shouldn't be listened to uncritically, either. However, I would pay attention. If you only watch Fox News, you will get a skewed version of events. The Fox News Channel prime time line-up often ignores bad news for the President (such as developments in the Mueller investigation) and pursues something else to distract you from allegations that hurt the President. The result is people who rely on Fox News for their news might as well be getting it from an alternate reality.

Either find a fairly well-respected mainstream news source such as USA Today or check the Google News page to find what stories are trending.

It's important to read stories, not just the headlines. Today's headlines scream about stories that are far less sensational when you get the full story. If you don't have time to read a news story, then don't fret or get angry about the headline until you have time to understand the issue.

When reading stories, ask questions about their credibility.

Does the reporter offer evidence to support this claim?

For example, a 2018 story for the New York Times reported the allegations of the daughter of a podiatrist who said her deceased father had diagnosed President Trump with bone spurs to avoid the draft in exchange for favorable treatment from the Trump family on property he rented from them. Nine paragraphs in, the reporter indicated no written evidence showed Trump had ever seen this podiatrist and no one outside the podiatrist's family confirmed it. Even members of the podiatrist's family had no firsthand knowledge and were only sharing what they said the podiatrist said.

What are the credibility of the sources?

When a source is named, ask if this person is credible. When a source is anonymous, evaluate how much you're being asked to believe by people who won't go on the record. This is not to say all anonymous sources are false. Sometimes, sources who work for the White House are anonymous because they're not allowed to speak the truth on-the-record and they want to get the truth out. However, anonymous sources may also be gossips speaking out of frustration or jealousy. They may be misleading the reporter up with a false story, so their boss can proclaim, "Fake news!" Information obtained from an anonymous source needs to be taken with a grain of salt, and the more a story relies on anonymous sources, the larger that grain should be.

What are the reporters' biases?

Once, "News" and "Opinion" were two separate spheres of journalism. Today, we have advocacy journalists whose ideology flows off the page. In some cases, it's obvious a reporter wants to not just tell you the facts, but how to think about the facts. However, subtler notes can be picked up on, such as buzzwords that betray an ideological bias. In addition, ask if the journalist gave both sides a fair amount time while examining each side of the story. That a reporter is biased doesn't necessarily mean their story is false. However, the story may have angles they can't see because of their particular biases.

Is what you're reading news or narrative?

Consider the example of a November 2013 story in which a lesbian New Jersey waitress produced a note stating, "I'm sorry I cannot tip because I don't agree with your lifestyle and how you live your life." The story was covered nationally and became a cause celeb with many lamenting how unloving and unkind Christians were to the LGBT community.

It turned out the waitress had altered the bill. The couple never wrote the note, and in fact gave the waitress a twenty percent tip. Aside from the story's falsehood, the question is why it became a national news story. On its face, it's the story of diners treating a waitress badly, which is a sadly common event. The reason it made news is that a fit narrative the mainstream media advances.

The media ignores stories that don't fit their narratives. For example, it ignores stories of misconduct by abortionists including the notorious Dr. Kermit Gosnell, whose incompetence caused the deaths of several women and who illegally killed born-alive infants. Similarly, many alt-right outlets will elevate any story of crimes committed by Hispanic immigrants or Muslim refugees to the level of national news to forward their racist narrative.

Narrative journalism is not about the truth but about confirming the story of your own ideology. The narratives tend to be broad and either false or mix in falsehood. Don't buy a narrative unless you've thoroughly researched it.

It's also important to address the role talk radio plays in our lives. First of all, not all talk radio is created equal. Many critiques of talk radio paint with too broad a brush. Some radio interview shows help inform people and allow them to connect with their elected officials and other newsmakers. Some serious-minded shows address real local and national political issues in an honest way. And quite a bit of talk radio is not about politics at all.

However, some political talk radio programs do thrive on making people afraid and angry and keeping them that way. These shock jocks say things to rile people up. Further, these talk radio programs peddle propaganda for the RNC. They either view their program as a way to get personal political power or they worship political power for Republicans as the highest good.

Programs in these categories are worth cutting back or eliminating from your life. That especially goes for the ones that spread fear and anger. Back in 2004, I used to listen to one of these shows on my fifteen-minute commute home and I would listen to a particular host, and he would get people angry and he would be entertaining in the process. However, I found I arrived home every night in a foul mood. Once I turned him off, that problem went away.

To replace the anger-inducing, propaganda-shouting talk radio, try to find good programs on your radio dial. Also try good podcasts. Lots of informative, political podcasts are not as shouty or as partisan as their radio counterparts. National Review includes podcasts hosted by Jonah Goldberg, Jay Nordlinger, and David French and Alexandra DeSanctis. There's a podcast by Commentary Magazine and one by the new conservative website, The Bulwark.

Becoming a better news consumer is like becoming a healthier food consumer. It involves cutting the junk out of your life and replacing it with healthy alternatives.

On a related note, seek to become better in the way you use social media to discuss politics, if you choose to do so at all. There are many valid personal and professional reasons that people choose to not talk about politics on their social media accounts and that's fine. It can take up a lot of energy and distract from more productive things.

If you choose to participate, there are a few things to watch out for. First, watch how much time and energy you spend debating politics on social media. It can be time-consuming and emotionally draining. Few opinions are changed online and almost no one's mind is changed in the string of a long comments section. It is fine to take two to five minutes to respond to something every now and again, but it's a waste of time and energy to spend half an hour or more responding to comments on an issue. If you have any talent for political writing, you could spend your time better by starting your own blog or publishing a post on medium.com about your thoughts on a particular issue where it'll be read by more people.

Second, it's important to be careful about the news stories you share on social media. If you're being a smart news consumer, then you'll have a lot of good articles to share from your own reading, but you may also see articles on other people's timelines that look worth discussing. Before sharing, it's important to make sure the article is true and timely.

It has been said a lie travels halfway around the world while the truth is putting on its boots. The lie will cross the globe several times in our misinformation age. If you see a story on someone's timeline, read the whole thing before sharing it and make sure the story is valid.

Don't be like people who post a dubious story with a note saying, "I wonder if this is true." By sharing it on their timeline, they've helped its algorithm and guaranteed more people will see it and read the story without noting the question. It says to others, "Could you use a search engine for me?" which hurts your credibility.

If you don't have time to check a story, then you don't have time to share it. Save it and check on it when you do have time. In addition, a good rule of thumb is, if you're not sure if a news story is true, it probably isn't. Listen to your intuition and don't share the story without checking it.

Be on the alert for satire. Satire is not fake news, as it's not meant to be taken at face value. The Onion and the Babylon Bee are the best-known satire sites. However, there are lesser known satire sites. None mean to be taken as fact, but they are by those not paying attention. If someone is outraged by a headline, check the source. If it's a known satire website, then gently inform the poster its satire. If a site is unfamiliar, click the link and examine the site. You'll either find a general satire disclosure, or you'll be able to tell from the other articles published. If you opt to choose to share satire from a lesser known site, be sure to include a satire warning.

Another thing to check is when the story occurred. I've seen a story be shared with the person assuming it is a current news item when it is several years old. In many cases, it's a threat that has been resolved. As such, it's important to check the date stamp.

For example, early in the Trump Administration, Ford Motors decided to cancel building a new plant in Mexico and to expand operations in the U.S. That story pops up on my Facebook news feed multiple times each week when it occurred nearly two years ago. A casual news reader may think it's a current story. A very inattentive one may think Ford has canceled many planned expansions into Mexico, all thanks to Trump.

Also, beware of memes. Memes can be funny, clever, or give a perceived smack down to political foes. In reality, political memes oversimplify issues, spread disinformation, and unfairly attack their agenda's opponents as idiots. Some memes bare an uncanny resemblance to propaganda posters made by totalitarian regimes in the first half of the twentieth century. Those posters dehumanized disfavored groups, spread disinformation, and exalted "the leader."

In addition, two reports by the Senate Intelligence Committee showed that memes and videos were used by Russia's Internet Research Agency to "sow discord in the U.S. political system" according to a report by USA Today. The memes Russia's IRA produced were shared by more than thirty million people. This is one reason to be cautious in what you share. What patriotic American wants to be the unwitting agent of a hostile power?

This doesn't mean we should engage in a new red scare. Not every divisive, inaccurate, dehumanizing meme is produced by paid trolls operating out of Russia. The fact is far too many Americans are willing to help the Russian's achieve their goals for nothing.

Avoid joining online mobs. Social media tempts us to offer our takes on matters before we have all the facts. This behavior has ruined lives and businesses. Don't make a judgment based on a snippet of a video or a picture. Follow the Golden Rule. Let the evidence come in before you make a judgment. No one has ever regretted waiting for more facts but many have regretted rushing to judgment.

In online interactions, it's important to be respectful. This is a challenge, given the emotionally-charged nature of our politics. However, if we want to be part of the solution, we need to strive to be decent in our conversation. We may mess up and step over the line because we're flawed human beings, but we shouldn't make incivility, harshness, and vindictiveness our default operating position. If we do, we're adding to the problem rather than solving it.

Let's avoid making harsh judgments about others, particularly people we don't know. Focus upon the argument/behavior, not the person. At the same time, be selective about who we engage with online. The Internet is crawling in trolls who thrive on bringing out the worst in others. The saying, "Don't feed the trolls," is a good rule to live by. When it becomes clear someone is trolling you, don't let them pull you down to their level.

Social media platforms come with options like "Block," "Mute," and "Unfollow." Learn to use these, and use them well, to avoid unproductive and unprofitable conversations.

Regardless of the sloppy, lazy, or dishonest practices others use on social media, be a person of integrity in the way that you manage your social media accounts. Be a person your friends trust to be respectful to everyone, shoot straight, and never spread falsehood, not even to advance your worthy cause. That credibility is a precious commodity in the world these days.

In short, there's a lot we can do to address the issues I've covered in this book. I believe we can all make a great difference, if we all consider what we can do and then do our part.

Final Thoughts

In this book, I've critiqued the Republicans, Democrats, Libertarians, the Constitution Party, and nascent concept parties such as the American Federalist Party and Federalist Party. However, I want to be fair. All of these parties' membership includes patriotic or sincere people. I just disagree with many of their behaviors strongly.

Some are staying in the GOP, trying to save the GOP from Trumpism and from the GOP itself. I respect that commitment and the willingness to stand for unpopular beliefs in the GOP. However, the GOP has crossed the threshold and is beyond salvage.

I respect the accomplishments of Libertarian and Constitution Parties as far as they've gone. They managed to get on the ballot in many states, so they could vote for candidates who reflect their values. I respect the hard work required to sustain and achieve that. However, I can't pretend they are a viable vehicle for promoting the values they champion.

Individuals in new parties have stepped forward to offer Americans a new choice in the Federalist and American Federalist Parties. I respect that undertaking. It takes time, commitment, and patriotism. Yet, I see major flaws in their strategies and they've failed to take organizational steps that would mark a serious party. As of this writing, the Federalist Party appears to have gone dormant as it stopped making website posts in 2018 and currently their website resolves to an error. The American Federalist Party is still active. I'm open to them making changes to become the party America needs right now.

Across America, tens of millions of us are fed up with both major parties. That discontent was growing all through the 2016 elections. The question is what are we going to do about it?

The sleazy state of America's two powerful parties isn't the country's biggest problem. Many cultural, moral, spiritual, and social problems loom larger.

Yet no problem is improved by leaving America's governance to two corrupt political parties. Both are far too willing to ignore flagrantly unethical conduct and tear our country apart for political gain.

Most of us have been part of the problem, including me. It's so easy to get swept up in an angry mob and say things that are unwise or intemperate.

Voices in the political realm have become increasingly shrill as they spout crazy nonsense. It's easier to back away from the craziness rather than lovingly confront it with the truth. Whatever we have done in the past to contribute to the problem, we need to own our mistakes and become part of the solution.

In our current political environment, hope eludes many like an impossible dream. You may question if we can do any better, if we're capable of forming a party that will respect American ideals and American principles and present a positive vision for America. I believe the answer is that we can. The question is if we'll have the will to do it.

Grassroots citizens can create a political party that will defend America's core values, break down barriers, and reach out to the Americans offended by both political parties. We are Americans, heirs to the Constitution and the Bill of Rights and a system of government the like of which had never existed on the face of the Earth. Many predicted its failure, but it has stood the test of time. Even now, the Constitution protects us from the worst tendencies of our leaders and holds their passions in check, even though it has been battered.

The political elites and the lazy TV analysts will scoff at a new party and utter conventional wisdom about its demise. They will base their predictions on the dead and failing third parties that have come before us. Let us build a different party, one that can surprise them.

Let's show them all what Americans can do.

Acknowledgements

Thanks to my wife, Andrea, for her editing and formatting assistance. She is an invaluable partner and a great help to me.

I also honor those who feel homeless in our current corrupt two-party environment. I hope this book addresses your concerns and gives you hope for America's political future.

About the Author

Adam Graham was a state coordinator for three different presidential campaigns. He has served two terms as a precinct committeeman, he is the former Secretary of Flathead County (Montana) Republican Party, and he was a delegate to the 2008 Idaho Republican State Convention. He is also a former candidate for the Idaho Legislature.

He has written articles on US and Idaho politics for a variety of sources, including PJMedia.com and CaffeinatedThoughts.com, and he formerly wrote a blog on politics for the Idaho Press-Tribune.

Graham is also the author of the political detective novel *Slime Incorporated* as well as *Tales of the Dim Knight* and the Adventures of Powerhouse series of Superhero comedy novels. He and his wife Andrea live in Boise, Idaho with their dog, Rocky. They currently are seeking to adopt their first child.

Check Our New American Party

We Can Do Better, America is the beginning, not the end, of our conversation. We'll continue to advocate for a new political party that supports core conservative values that we've talked about in this book.

At *Our New American Party,* we'll share news and opinion and invite you to take part in the conversation. I'll also being adding a page where you can share why have left your old party or why you otherwise are looking for a new conservative party. In addition, we'll have a newsletter link. This page will not be an official homepage for a new political party but will certainly have news and commentary on developments in that direction.

Come and visit us at http://ournewamericanparty.com and be sure to sign up for my newsletter while you're there.

www.ingramcontent.com/pod-product-compliance
Lightning Source LLC
Chambersburg PA
CBHW031119250726
48655CB00004B/1766